1000 YEARS OF PERFECT JUSTICE

1000 YEARS OF PERFECT JUSTICE

JIMMY D. OGLE

TATE PUBLISHING
AND **ENTERPRISES**, LLC

1000 Years of Perfect Justice
Copyright © 2013 by Jimmy D. Ogle. All rights reserved.

No part of this publication may be reproduced, stored in a retrieval system or transmitted in any way by any means, electronic, mechanical, photocopy, recording or otherwise without the prior permission of the author except as provided by USA copyright law.

Scripture taken from the *New King James Version*. Copyright © 1982 by Thomas Nelson, Inc. Used by permission. All rights reserved.

The opinions expressed by the author are not necessarily those of Tate Publishing, LLC.

Published by Tate Publishing & Enterprises, LLC
127 E. Trade Center Terrace | Mustang, Oklahoma 73064 USA
1.888.361.9473 | www.tatepublishing.com

Tate Publishing is committed to excellence in the publishing industry. The company reflects the philosophy established by the founders, based on Psalm 68:11,
"The Lord gave the word and great was the company of those who published it."

Book design copyright © 2013 by Tate Publishing, LLC. All rights reserved.
Cover design by Allen Jomoc
Interior design by Mary Jean Archival

Published in the United States of America

ISBN: 978-1-62510-528-8
1. Religion / Biblical Criticism & Interpretation / New Testament
2. Religion / Biblical Studies / New Testament
12.12.06

CONTENTS

Foreword	9
Explanation of Terms	11
Doomsday Forecasters: The End of What?	15
The Pre-Rapture	23
The Rapture	33
If You Miss The Rapture	41
The Tribulation: Part 1	59
The Tribulation: Part 2	71
The Battle of Armageddon	89
1,000 Years of Perfect Justice	95
Why? Why?	117
The Great White Throne Judgment	121
I Make All Things New	125

DEDICATION

I dedicate this book to my wife of forty-nine years, Barbara Mignon (Taylor) Ogle.

FOREWORD

This book is titled *1,000 Years of Perfect Justice*, but it covers much more than the thousand-year reign of Christ.

It begins in the pre-Rapture era, which is where we are now and then goes to the Rapture of the church. It then deals with the Tribulation, the second coming of Jesus, his defeat of the antichrist, and the rescue of Israel. Jesus then sets up his earthly kingdom and reigns for one thousand years. The book then covers the Great White Throne Judgment, the new earth, and the new Jerusalem.

This book organizes pertinent Scriptures from the Old and New Testaments and puts them in an understandable order. This makes it easier for the reader to follow the flow of these latter-day events. After the church is raptured or "caught away," these other events will occur on an exact schedule. As one era ends, the next era will begin.

There is some overlap of Scripture and discussion because these eras do transition one after the other and, to a degree, intertwine with each other. Any overlap of Scripture or discussion will only reinforce the previous point.

I desire that the reader gain vital insights into what is going to happen as these events unfold. The Christian solution to these events is to be ready to meet Jesus when he comes for the church. Many, who perceive themselves to be Christians, will not be ready when Jesus comes.

Make sure that you have "oil in your lamp" and are expectant of his coming at any moment. No Scripture has to be fulfilled before Jesus comes for the church. It could happen at any time! There are Scriptures that show us when the time is near. Diligent Christians will be able to discern these signs. All this and more is dealt with in this book. Read on, and I hope you enjoy.

EXPLANATION OF TERMS

Christians may not need to have *church* or *Rapture* explained to them, but this book is for everyone, not just Christians. We will start with the church.

The Church. This is not the large building on main street with the steeple on top. It is not necessarily all the people who attend there. Being on the membership roll of a church does not ensure that you are a member of the church that Jesus is coming for. It is good to attend church and to be an active member. The word tells us to "not forsake" the assembling of ourselves together but exhort one another, especially as we see the "day" approaching. The day we see approaching refers to the Rapture of the church.

The Church that Jesus comes back for consists of all people, worldwide, who have accepted Jesus as their savior. They have believed with their hearts and confessed with their mouths that Jesus Christ is the Son of God. They believe that he died of his own free will as a sacrifice for mankind. They believe that he rose on the third day and now sits on the right hand of the Father in heaven, making intercession for us.

Every nation on earth has Christian citizens, even in Islamic countries and countries who claim no god. Many of these people have not had the opportunity to attend regular church services or have their names on a membership roll. It makes no difference! They are members of the church that Jesus is coming for.

Jesus will show no preference to denominations such as Baptist, Methodist, Presbyterian, etc. Many members from all denominations will be included in the Rapture, but many church members will not be included. The criterion for meeting Jesus in the air is that you are a born-again believer, living for Jesus. I recently heard a pastor say that he was "Baptist born and Baptist bred, and when he died, he would be Baptist dead." It got a chuckle from the audience, but the truth will be does Jesus know you, or will you hear, "depart from me, I never knew you?" Jesus is coming for the ones that he knows. The church is all of the born-again believers from all over the world. This is what I am referring to when you see church in this book.

The Rapture. Okay, okay, the word *rapture* is not in the Bible. The best translation is a catching or snatching away. The term *rapture*, however, is a good description of what happens on that day. The dictionary defines *rapture* as the state of being carried away with great joy, love, ecstasy, or pleasure. It can be in body or spirit. *Rapture* is a good description of what happens when Jesus redeems his church. I will use it many times in this book. The Rapture refers to Jesus's catching away of his church. The Christians are taken and the non-Christians are left. The Christians will be instantly glorified and meet Jesus in the air. This is what I mean every time you see *rapture* in this book. The Rapture of the church is covered in chapter 3.

The Antichrist or the beast. These two names are referring to the same person. He will be the world ruler during the Tribulation. I don't know what he will call himself, but the Scriptures refer to him as the antichrist or the beast. He will definitely be opposed to Christ. The spirit of the antichrist is already at work through false teachers and false apostles. We will discuss them in chapter 2. The person that will rise up as the world leader is probably already grown and will arise out of the Old Persian Empire. That area now consists of Syria, Iraq, Iran, Russia, and eastern Europe.

The Antichrist or the beast will rule the world during the last three and a half years of the Tribulation. After the battle of Armageddon, he will be cast into the lake of fire.

The Tribulation. This refers to the last seven years on earth prior to Jesus's second coming. The last three and a half years will be the worst. It will be a time of great suffering and punishment for earth's inhabitants. The Tribulation is covered in chapter 5.

The battle of Armageddon. This is a misunderstood event. There will be no losses for the Army of heaven, but all the followers of the antichrist will perish. The battle of Armageddon is addressed in chapter 6.

The thousand-year reign. Refers to the last one thousand years of this earth. A new earth will then be created. Jesus will establish his kingdom on this earth and rule in righteousness for one thousand years. There will be no sin or anything that can hurt or make you afraid. The wolf will lay down with the lamb, the lion will eat straw, and small children will play with snakes. A river will flow from under the throne of Jesus, and the water will heal everything that it touches. The thousand-year reign is covered in chapter 7.

The saints or the elect. When mentioned in this book, it refers to the people of the nation of Israel. Christians are referred to as saints or elect in the New Testament, but all Christians will be raptured prior to the Tribulation. There will be people on earth that will become Christians during the Tribulation. Multitudes will be executed for their testimony. Millions of Christians will survive the Tribulation and enter the thousand-year reign as followers of Jesus.

The Christians who have gone on are saints. The Christians who convert during the Tribulation are saints. However, the saints or elect spoken of in this book will be referring to the people of Israel.

DOOMSDAY FORECASTERS: THE END OF WHAT?

> Question: What do doomsday forecasters say when they predict the end of the world and nothing happens?
>
> Answer: With a shrug, "Oh well, it's not the end of the world."

The world will end on such and such a day. We have all heard it, and it creates concern among lots of people. The next date that you may hear is December 21, 2012. The Mayan calendar ends on that day.

These doomsday forecasters do us no actual harm, but their predictions do contribute to misunderstanding of this subject. They set dates for the world or time to come to an end. They view both as the same thing. Anyone predicting the end of the world or the end of time simply does not understand the Scriptures.

What do they think is going to happen when the world "comes to an end?" Is everyone going to die in a huge fireball? What will God do then? Does he create a new earth with new people and start over? There is nothing in the word of God that suggests the world will come to a sudden, apocalyptic end. The idea is ludicrous. Jesus warned the Sadducees in Matthew 22:29, "You do greatly err, not knowing the Scriptures." This also applies to the doomsday forecasters of today as they continue to predict the end of the world.

God has a great plan for mankind. He will bring all of it to fulfillment in an orderly and systematic fashion. The sudden, cataclysmic end of the world is not in the word of God!

The next major event that is prophesied in the word of God is the Rapture or catching away of the church. Christians, both dead and alive, will be changed in the twinkling of an eye and meet Jesus in the air. But it is not the end of the world! Life on earth will continue, but without the benefit of Christians. They are gone.

After the church is caught away, the Tribulation will begin. Conditions on earth will get worse for seven years with the last three and a half years being the most grievous. The world will be in total ruin by the end of the Tribulation. Conditions will be so bad that life could not continue on earth unless the Tribulation ended. This will be covered in chapter 5 – part 2.

Living conditions on earth will be abhorrent during the last three and a half years of the Tribulation, but Jesus assures us in Matthew 24 that it will end. When the Tribulation ends, it is not the end of the world! Relax, the world will continue for another one thousand years.

Jesus will return after the Tribulation. He will destroy the forces of the antichrist and cast the beast and false prophet into the lake of fire. Jesus will then begin his earthly rule, but it is not the end of the world! Relax, the end is not near.

Time will end after one thousand years are completed, but what happens when time comes to an end? Answer: we no longer keep track of time. We go into eternity where time is not relevant. This earth will come to an end after one thousand years are completed, but what happens? Answer: after it is emptied of people, it will be recreated into a new and perfect earth. This earth will "melt with fervent heat," but no one will be here when it happens.

Where will everyone be? Answer: after one thousand years have ended, all of the unrighteous are in hell. They will be delivered up before God to be judged. This is covered in chapter 9. All of the righteous are with Jesus in heaven. There are no people on earth. It is now ready to "melt with fervent heat" and be recreated into that new and perfect earth which Peter spoke of.

Hell is now located in the inner parts of this earth. It will be relocated and cast into the lake of fire before the new and perfect earth is created.

In 2 Peter 3:10, it tells us how the earth will be recreated. This is also where the doomsday folks get the idea of a giant fireball. "The heavens will pass away with a great noise, and the elements will melt with fervent heat; both the earth and the works that are in it will be burned up."

Peter then tells us that according to his promise, there will be a new earth with new heavens.

The word tells us that this earth will come to an end. It will be burned with fire and melt with fervent heat. It will not happen like a "bolt out of the blue," but will happen in the process of God's overall plan. The new and perfect earth will be a wonderful creation unlike anything we can imagine. We will have free access to it throughout eternity.

The apostle John saw a new heaven and a new earth. The first heaven and the first earth had passed away, and there was no more sea. Note that the new heaven spoken of is not the heaven where God resides. That heaven will remain eternally. The new heavens spoken of here will consist of the atmosphere, sky, stars, and whatever else surrounds the new earth. I have heard it preached that we will spend eternity in heaven, and I have heard it preached that we will live on the new earth throughout eternity. The truth is, we will have free access to both. Genesis 28:12 tells us about Jacob's ladder. "Then he dreamed and behold, a ladder was set up on earth, and its top reached to heaven; and the angels of God were ascending and descending on it." Jacob was given this vision in a dream in the genesis of time. This dream will be fulfilled after time has ended. There will be no ladder, and the beings that Jacob perceived to be angels of God will also include the saints of God. Jesus tells us in Matthew 22:30, "In the resurrection, we are like the angels of God in heaven."

How will we ascend and descend between heaven and earth? We will fly like the angels do now. I have almost twelve thousand hours of flying time as pilot in command, but it has all been in helicopters. I will someday fly freely as a glorified being. It will be the ultimate way to fly. I get goose bumps when I think about it.

Let's get back to "the end" as it is used in Scripture. The end tends to conjure dread in our minds, especially the end of time. There is no need for dread. We will now look to Scriptures that tell us in no uncertain terms that there is no end.

Isaiah 9:7 says, "Of the increase of his government and peace, there shall be no end." In Luke 1:33, angels declare at Jesus's birth, "Of His kingdom there shall be no end." Ephesians 3:21 tells us, "To him be the glory in the church by Jesus Christ throughout all ages, world without end."

Fifty million years from now, although we will not be keeping time, all of the righteous will still be living gloriously with Christ, and the unrighteous will still be suffering torment in the lake of fire.

Here is another scriptural use of the end. Matthew 10:22 says, "He who endures to the end will be saved." Hebrews 3:6 says, "We are of the house of Christ if we hold fast the confidence of hope firm to the end." There are several other Scriptures that speak of holding our faith, hope, trust, confidence, or other beliefs to the end. The end referenced here is the end of our life.

If we are raptured, that would also be the end of our physical bodies. We are told in 1 Corinthians 15:53 that "our mortal body must put on immortality." When our mortal body puts on immortality, it will go through the death process to get there. However, this change will happen in the twinkling of an eye. It will be over before we realize what happened.

In Matthew 24:3, the disciples ask Jesus, "What will be the sign of your coming and the end of the age?" Jesus is still answering the question in verse 14, and says, "First must this gospel be preached in all the world, as a witness to all nations, then the end will come." The end spoken of here is the end End of the age. The end of this age will occur at the end of the Tribulation. The thousand-year reign will be this earth's last age.

The gospel must be preached in all the world. This sounds like the great commission to go unto the world to preach, teach, and make disciples. I have heard it preached that it would take sixty to seventy million missionaries to fulfill this commission, and that it has to be done prior to the Rapture. Wrong! This has nothing to do with the great commission. The church will already be gone when this prophecy is fulfilled. No missionaries will be available. This gospel message that must be preached in all the world— to all nations—will be preached by angels just prior to the end of the Tribulation. The verse says, "Then the end will come." The word *"first"* throws us a slight curve, but it plainly indicates there are only two things to do: (1) preach the gospel to every person on earth and (2) bring the age to an end. God's word tells us in Revelation 14:6–7 how this will be accomplished.

> I saw another angel flying in heaven, having the everlasting gospel to preach to those who dwell on earth; to every tribe, nation, people, and tongue, saying, fear God and give glory to him, for the hour of his judgment has come!

Having what? The everlasting gospel!
To what? Preach!
To who? Those who dwell on earth!
Saying what? Fear God and give glory to him!
Why? His judgment is at hand!

This Scripture is fulfilled by angels. They will ensure that no one is missed. Those in caves, in jungles, or on remote islands will not be missed. Every person will hear the gospel message preached by an angel. They will hear in their own language. The angels will fly the length and breadth of the earth with voices booming like thunder. Everyone will hear and understand the message and will have the opportunity to cry out to God. Millions will accept, but millions more will reject this message. It will be their last chance for salvation. Millions of missionaries could not ensure that everyone on earth heard this gospel message. This final gospel message has to be preached by angels, and according to God's word, it is.

We conclude by the word of God that there is no end. There are transition points through the ages where we go from one stage of God's great plan into the next. Almost two thousand years ago, we transitioned from the law to grace, and the church age began. When the church is raptured, the Tribulation will begin. When the Tribulation ends, the thousand-year reign of Jesus begins. When the thousand-year reign ends, time will end. The earth will then be recreated into a new and perfect earth.

Jesus tells us to "fear not" and "let not your hearts be troubled." Believe in Jesus and his word and doomsday prophets will be meaningless to you. Try not to laugh at their predictions. They are misguided and need a better understanding of God's word.

We are exhorted, no, commanded, to study the word of God. We study to show ourselves approved unto God, a workman who needs not be ashamed, rightly dividing the word of truth.

We combat all false prophecies and teachings with the truth of God's word. Be diligent about your study. Make it a priority for your life and begin to feel a sense of urgency about it. All Scripture is inspired by God. It will ground you with sound doctrine. It will correct you in this life. It will instruct you in righteousness. The word of God furnishes you with everything you need to live a successful life. Doomsday forecast wilt in the light of God's word. Make the word the center of your life.

THE PRE-RAPTURE

Take heed that no one deceive you

Matthew 24:3-4

In Matthew 24:3, Jesus was asked by his disciples for the sign of his coming. His first words to them in verse 4 are, "Take heed that no one deceives you. For many will come in my name, saying, I am the Christ and deceive many." They will come in the name of Jesus and will deceived many! It's where we are now (2012). Doctrinal deceptions will be rampant just prior to the Rapture of the church. Satan's desire is to turn God's people from the truth.

Another translation of the phrase, "I am the Christ," comes out, "I am of Christ." These deceivers will claim that what they teach is the truth. They will claim to be Christians but will imply that they a have greater understanding of God than fundamentalists do. Fundamentalists are those folks who believe what the word of God says.

The most important thing for Christians to be aware of in the pre-Rapture era is these false teachers and false apostles. They will claim to represent God. Their message will sound good. They will have an appearance of righteousness but will deny the power thereof. False teachers will appeal to those individuals who have "itching ears." Those who do not want to hear about sin, repentance, the cross, the blood of Jesus, or any other sound doctrine want everything to be easy. They do not want to feel conviction for sin or for salvation. They are "goldilocks" Christians. They want everything "just right."

The modern-day false teachers are those described in 2 Timothy 3:5, "Having a form of godliness but denying the power there of, from such, *turn away*!" These false teachers never mention the name of Jesus or the Holy Spirit. That is how they deny the power thereof. The power is in the name of Jesus and through the Holy Spirit. These false teachers will have a form of godliness. They will look and act like Christians. Some will be pastors. They will use any media to promote their doctrine but seem to prefer local newspapers. Some of the more literate have written books. In 2 Peter 2:18, it says of them, "They speak great, swelling words of emptiness and allure through the lust of the flesh, the ones who have actually escaped from those who live in error." This verse warns us that Christians, those who have escaped, are being lured away by these false doctrines. The goal of false teachers is (1) lure the Christian back into the world and (2) prevent the nonbeliever from hearing the truth of God's word.

In 2 Thessalonians 2:10, it warns us about "unrighteous deceptions coming from those who perish because they do not receive the truth." What is the truth?

In John 14:6, Jesus said, "I am the way, the truth, and the Life. NO ONE comes to the Father except through me." This is the truth that saves people. Jesus is the way. No one comes to God except through Jesus. Jesus is the mediator between God and man. Whatever you pray, ask in the name of Jesus. False teachers will accuse you of being narrow-minded if you say Jesus is the only way to salvation.

False teachers attempt to legitimize other religions by saying that all religions ultimately pray to or acknowledge the same God. False teachers will accuse you of excluding other religions from salvation or access to God if you teach that Jesus is the only way. The truth is, we are not excluding anyone from salvation. We are telling them how to be saved and that Jesus died for all humanity. Jesus can be accepted by all, including Hindus, Buddhists, and other religions of the world. I will point out that when you accept Jesus as your savior, you will no longer be a Hindu or a Buddhist. You will be a Christian. God desires that everyone know the truth and Jesus is *the truth*. John 8:32 says, "The truth shall make you free." No other religion on earth makes you free. They all include works to arrive at salvation. Salvation through faith in Jesus Christ is the free gift of God. Christians are saved by what they believe, not by what they do. Ephesians 2:8–9 says, "By grace are you saved, by faith, not of yourselves, it is the gift of God, not of works, lest anyone should boast."

In actuality, there are two spiritual beliefs: Christianity and everything else. Everything else is anti-Christianity. In 1 John 2:22–23, it says, "He is a liar who denies that Jesus is the Christ. He is an antichrist who denies the Father and the Son. He who denies the Son does not have the Father but he who acknowledges the Son has the Father also." Anyone who denies that Jesus Christ is the Son of God will not be saved. Acts 4:12 tells us, "There is salvation in no other, for there is no other name under heaven given among men by which we can be saved."

False teachers pervert the Scriptures in a number of ways. One of their techniques is to quote part of a Scripture and omit the rest of the verse. They can then distort it anyway they please. Here are some examples of distorted Scriptures that you have seen or will see:

Example 1

John 3:16 says, "For God so loved the world." False teachers stop here. They then make any point they want to. They say that God loves all the world, not just Christians. It says it right here. We are all covered by God's love and nothing bad will happen. They distort the Scripture and try to make it say something else. This appeals to the flesh and draws many away from sound doctrine. The verse reads, "For God so loved the world that he (what) gave his only begotten Son, (why) that whosoever believes in him should (what) not perish, but have everlasting life."

This tells us that if we believe in Jesus, we will not perish, but have everlasting life. The opposite is also true. If you do not believe in Jesus, you will not have everlasting life. John 3:18 says, "He who believes on him is not condemned; But he who believes not is *condemned already*, because he has not believed in the name of the only begotten Son of God."

Jesus says in Matthew 7:21–23,

> Not every one who says Lord, Lord, will enter into the kingdom of heaven but he who does the will of the Father in heaven. Many will say to me in that day, Lord, Lord, have we not prophesied in your name? And in your name cast out devils? And in your name done many wonderful works?

Many false teachers are deceived themselves and think they are doing wonderful "works" for the Lord. Jesus says to them in verse 23, "Depart from me you who work iniquity, I never knew you."

These people looked like Christians, sounded like Christians, deceived many into believing they were Christians, but Jesus says to them, "I never knew you." They had never accepted Jesus as their savior. The criterion for entry into heaven is, Does Jesus know you? Have you believed in your heart and confessed with your mouth that Jesus Christ is Lord?

John 3:36 warns, "He who does not believe in the Son of God shall not see life, but the wrath of God abides on him."

Example 2

John 3:17 says, "God did not send his Son into the world to condemn the world." False teachers stop here. They then say that if God did not send his son into the world to condemn the world, then no one is condemned. But the rest of the verse tells us that the world through him might be saved. Again, all the people of the world can be saved by believing in their heart that Jesus Christ is the Son of God and confessing it with their mouth. Can it be that simple? Yes! Believe and confess. The confession is absolutely necessary. This is another power that false teachers want to deny. Many of our churches today have members who have never made this confession.

Example 3

Second Peter 3:9 says, "The Lord is not willing that any should perish." False teachers stop here. They then smugly proclaim that if it is not God's will that anyone will perish, then no one is going to perish. Is God really God they ask?

Does God get what he wants? Yes, they proclaim, and therefore, no one is going to perish because the word just said that it is not God's will that any should perish. Case closed, they say. The rest of the verse tells us, "But that all should come to *repentance*." *Repentance* is a word that false teachers do not want to hear or acknowledge. God desires that all of mankind come to repentance, and I will say to false teachers, *repent*!

Example 4

Romans 8:28 says, "All things work together for good." False teachers stop here. They then claim that this says everything will work out good for everybody and there is no reason for concern. God says he will work it out good for all of us. The rest of the verse says, "To those who love the Lord and are called according to his purpose."

This is a wonderful promise that God has given to those who love him. No matter what your problem is, if you trust in the Lord, he will work it out for good. You can count on God's promises. They are rock-solid for those who love him.

Example 5

Last example, I promise. 1 Timothy 4:10 says, "God is the savior of all men." False teachers stop here. They then claim that all men are saved. There is nothing else to do. The rest of the verse tells us that we have to believe. False teachers deny the power of believing on the name of Jesus, but the word of God tells us over and over that we must believe on Jesus to be saved.

That was the last example, but false teachers can pervert any Scripture by misquoting, partial quoting, or taking it out of context. Satan distorted the Scripture three times in his effort to get Jesus to sin. How did Jesus combat this perversion of the Scripture? He answered Satan each time, "It is written!" Be on guard for these false teachings and doctrines. We are living in the beginning of sorrows spoken of by Jesus. I refer to this time as the pre-Rapture. Jesus charged us, "Take heed that no one deceive you!"

Jesus then warned of wars and rumors of wars, nation against nation, kingdom against kingdom, famines, pestilences, and earthquakes. He then exhorts us to "be not troubled for all these things must come to pass but the end is not yet." He then describes events that will occur during the Tribulation. The end of the Tribulation is the end of the age. It is also the end of the church age. That will be substantiated in chapter 5.

Jesus can come for his church at any time. Be ready.

Here are some things to watch for:

1. False teachers and apostles will proliferate. They are out in abundance right now.
2. War will be ongoing. Americans have become accustomed to war. We take it for granted. We have been at war since the attack on Pearl Harbor. World War II ended in 1945, and we went into Korea in 1948. We are still there. Then, came the cold war, Vietnam, Panama, Grenada, the first Gulf war and now, the war on terror with Iraq and Afghanistan. War is an integral part of America's history and heritage. It is also a sign that we are in the beginning of sorrows and very close to the Rapture of the church.
3. Earthquakes and other disasters will occur in all parts of the earth. Earthquakes that did enormous

damage in the last three or four years include Haiti, Christ Church in New Zealand, and Japan. There have been dozens of others. The recent tsunami in Japan was the worst ever recorded. Jesus said in Luke 21:25 that "the sea and waves would roar." I was reminded of this Scripture as I watched those horrific events on television. It's another sign of the time.

4. Men who have a form of godliness will teach that you can get rich by "moving the hand of God." 1 Timothy 6:5 says, "They will suppose that godliness is a means of gain." We went through this doctrine in the late eighties and early nineties. It went strong for about five years and then abated as people got wise to it. Some of this thinking is still hanging around today. If you haven't heard it yet, you will. The word of God tells us in the verse listed above, "From such, withdraw yourselves."

In 1 Timothy 4:1, it warns that "in the latter times some will depart from the faith, giving heed to deceiving spirits and doctrines of demons." These deceiving spirits and doctrines of demons will be using decent-looking, believable people to put forth their message. It will not be a red man with horns and a pitchfork. The verse above tells us that some will heed these deceiving spirits and depart from the faith. Christians departing from the faith has to happen prior to the rapture. It is the time we are in now, and it is happening now. In 2 Corinthians 11:13–15, it tells us:

> Such are false apostles, deceitful workers, transforming themselves into apostles of Christ. And no wonder! For Satan transforms himself into an Angel of Light. Therefore it is no great thing if his ministers also transform themselves into ministers of righteousness, whose end will be according to their works.

They will be "ministers." They will look good. They will stand behind church pulpits and preach a good-sounding message. They will be well-received by most, but beware, "their end will be according to their works." How can I know if they are real or false? The false will never tell you how to be saved, and they will tell you that your life will be wonderful. Just give money to their "ministry".

I give you one last exhortation. We are in the pre-Rapture era. We are very close to Jesus coming for the church. The main message that Jesus conveyed to the church and to Christians was: See that you be not troubled and take heed that no one deceive you. Take heed that no one deceive you! You can do it!

Satan desires to have you. He knows that his time is short. He is working furiously to subvert Christians from their faith. Give no place to Satan or his messengers. Stand strong in the word of God and in the power of Jesus Christ!

THE RAPTURE

Behold, I show you a mystery.

1 Corinthians 15:51–53

In 1 Corinthians 15:51–53, it says, "Behold, I show you a mystery. We shall not all sleep (die) but we shall all be changed, in a moment, in the twinkling of an eye, at the last trumpet." This is the first, last, and only trumpet that Christians will hear in this body of flesh. The trumpet judgments that sound during the Tribulation will not pertain to the raptured church. There is a very good likelihood that the trumpets will only be heard in heaven. That is where they are sounded, and nothing in the word indicates that the people on earth hear them. Now, the rest of the verse, "For the trumpet will sound, and the dead (in Christ) shall be raised incorruptible, and we (Christians who are alive) shall be changed. For this corruptible (flesh) must put on incorruption, and this mortal (our body) must put on immortality."

People in apostle Paul's day believed in the resurrection of the dead but had no concept of Jesus coming for the church. This was a new thing when Paul, through the Holy

Spirit, "showed them this mystery." A mystery is anything that was not previously known.

The change from mortal to immortal, from corruptible to incorruptible, will happen so fast, in a twinkling of an eye, that it will be over before we realize what happened. What a wonderful way to transition from this life to the next! Then it's up, up, and away to meet Jesus in the air!

Jesus said in John 14:2–3:

> In my fathers house are many mansions; if it were not so, I would have told you. I go to prepare a place for you. And if I go and prepare a place for you, I will come again and receive you unto myself; that where I am, there you may be also.

I will come back and receive you unto myself. What a beautiful Scripture! What did our Lord just say to us? He has gone back to heaven and prepared a place for us.

Verse 2 says a mansion, and I say a mansion unlike anything we can imagine. It is heaven after all, and even the streets are made of pure gold. He then tells us that he will come back and "receive us unto himself." Every time I think of this, I envision Jesus giving every one of us a warm embrace and perhaps a holy kiss. A kiss was the custom when Jesus walked on earth, and remember, we are the bride of Christ. The first thing that is going to happen when we get to heaven is the wedding supper of the Lamb. I cannot say anything else about it because the Scripture says nothing else about it. I know nothing else about it, but I do know this: Jesus promised us in the verse above that "where he was, we would be also." Jesus and his bride will always be together. Thank you, Jesus!

I love the idea of Jesus "receiving me unto himself."

The old gospel song says, "What a day that will be when my Jesus I shall see." I get goose bumps thinking about it.

Cheer up! Get enthused! When Jesus receives us unto himself, all of life's struggles and heartaches are over, all tears wiped away, all things will be new!

The church is the bride of Christ, and Jesus will have his bride with him throughout eternity. When he returns for the thousand-year reign, we will be with him. When he returns to heaven after the thousand-year reign, we will be there. In 1 Thessalonians 4:17 says, "Thus shall we ever be with the Lord."

When the Rapture of the church occurs, it will be amazing and spectacular, to say the least, and it will happen "in the twinkling of an eye." Yet very few people seem to be concerned or care about this fantastic occurrence. Do they simply not believe? Are they absorbed in the "affairs of this world?" Does it seem like a fairy tale? Or is some of it what was prophesied according to 2 Peter 3:3–4, which says, "Scoffers will come in the last days, walking according to their own lust, and saying, where is the promise of his coming? All things continue as they were from the beginning of creation."

Jesus warns us that he is coming at a time when we do not expect him. Non-Christians and many Christians are not expecting Jesus to return. Jesus then tells us, Christians, to always watch and be ready for his coming.

The word tells us there is a crown of righteousness for those who love his appearing. Do you love his appearing? Does the fact that Jesus could come at any moment excite or thrill you? I exhort you to be in anticipation of Jesus's return. It can happen at any moment. Expect it and make it real in your life. The word reassures us that we are not in darkness. That day should not come upon us as a thief. We are not appointed to wrath or hell, but to obtain salvation through our Lord Jesus Christ.

It is possible for Christians to see the day approaching. It is almost two thousand years closer than it was when the apostle Paul wrote these words. Paul thought it would happen in his day. I am sixty-nine years old and am persuaded that it will happen while I am still alive.

In 1 Thessalonians 4:14–17, it tells us that we will meet Jesus in the air, "For if we believe that Jesus died and rose again (this is a prerequisite for salvation), even so, God will bring with him those who sleep in Jesus." He will bring their soul and spirit to be reunited with their new and glorified bodies. When we die, our flesh returns to the earth and our spirit returns to God.

Continuing with Thessalonians:

> For this we say to you by the word of the Lord, that we who are alive and remain until the coming of the Lord will by no means precede those who are asleep. For the Lord himself will descend from heaven with a shout, with the voice of an archangel, and with the trumpet of God, and the dead in Christ shall rise first. Then we who are alive and remain shall be caught up together with them in the clouds to meet the Lord in the air. Thus shall we always be with the Lord!

When Jesus comes back for the church, he will not come all the way down to earth, but we will be "caught up" and meet him in the air and clouds. When Jesus ascended into heaven, a cloud received him out of the disciples' sight. Angels standing by informed the disciples that Jesus would return in the same manner that they had seen him go. Jesus will be obscured by the clouds and will not be seen by the people left on earth. He will be seen plainly by the ascending Christians, and they will be exhilarated to the maximum.

Do not confuse Jesus's coming for the church with his second coming. Scriptures concerning these two events are often intertwined and have to be separated. Scripture must be spiritually discerned. We are instructed that the natural man cannot receive the things of the spirit of God

They are foolishness to him. He cannot know them because they are *spiritually discerned*. The natural man cannot discern spiritual things, but the Christian can.

God's spirit resides in Christians. We are led by it, taught by it, and discern Scripture by it. The Holy Spirit teaches us the word of God.

Jesus will come for his church prior to the Tribulation. He will not touch down on earth. We will meet him in the air. That is the Rapture.

The Tribulation will end, and then Jesus will arrive with power and great glory. It will be like the lightning coming from the east and flashing to the west. Every eye will see him, every knee shall bow, and every tongue shall confess that Jesus Christ is Lord. That is the second coming.

During the thousand-year reign of Jesus and forever, there will be no other religions or beliefs. All those who opposed Jesus are destroyed at the battle of Armageddon, and the antichrist and the false prophet are cast into the lake of fire.

The other followers of the antichrist, from all nations on earth, will be judged at the judgment of the nations and cast directly into hell. Everyone left is a follower and worshiper of Jesus. At the end of the thousand-year reign, Satan will be let loose for a final uprising against Jesus. This will be dealt with in chapter 8.

I believe that any moment, I could be on my way up, seeing Jesus with outstretched arms, waiting for me and for all those who "love his appearing." I was given a vision of this in a dream. I saw Jesus and was going up to meet him in the air. As I went up, I gained speed, going faster and faster and feeling great exhilaration. As I was about to reach Jesus, I woke up. I remember bouncing on the bed. I must have been in the air, at least a little, and fell back down on the bed. I also remember extreme disappointment that it was not the real thing. It was the real thing during the vision. I thank God for it.

Jesus describes Lot's escape out of Sodom as a type of Rapture and then cautions us to "remember Lot's wife." She looked back and did not make it to safety. We also have the example of Peter getting out of the boat and going to Jesus. When he took his eyes off Jesus, he began to sink.

The Rapture of the church will happen very fast. We will be changed and on our way up " in the twinkling of an eye." Suddenly, you are going up, and you see Jesus. It will be possible to look back toward earth, but the spirit exhorted me to keep my eyes on Jesus. Focus in on Jesus and go to him!

After the apostle Paul explained the Rapture to us, he exhorted us to comfort one another with these words.

I hope these words are comforting to you. They are to me.

Next, we will determine if there is hope if you miss the Rapture. There is. However, I exhort you: be ready to meet Jesus at any time!

IF YOU MISS THE RAPTURE

(OH NO! I'M STILL HERE!)

After the church is raptured or "caught away" and you realize that you "missed the boat," so to speak, do understand that all is not lost. You, and everyone else left on earth, are in deep trouble, but it is still possible to be saved.

Jesus will continue to knock on the hearts of mankind, inviting them to be saved, and millions will be saved during the Tribulation. The choice will be clear-cut. Accept Jesus and be saved, or follow the antichrist and end up in hell. This will be dealt with fully in this chapter.

In Revelation 3:20, Jesus says, "Behold, I stand at the door and knock. If anyone hears my voice and opens the door, (Prays, Lord Jesus, come into my life) I will come into him and dine with him, and he with me."

Jesus did not cause this Scripture to be put in one of the Gospels as you might expect, but he caused it to be put in the Book of Revelation after he addressed the churches for the final time. The church will not be on earth during the Tribulation, and this will be the way to salvation. Respond when the spirit calls you! What does it mean that Jesus will come in and dine with me and me with him? When you feel the prompting of the Holy Spirit convicting you to accept Jesus, and you invite him in by believing in Jesus and praying, "Lord Jesus, come into my life," and anything else you feel led to pray, then Jesus will come in via the Holy Spirit. You will *feel* the Holy Spirit enter you, and you will know without a doubt that you are saved. Because God's Holy Spirit now resides in you, your body becomes the temple of God. In 1 Corinthians 6:19, it says, "Do you not know that your body is the temple of the Holy Spirit who is in you, whom you have from God, and you are not your own?"

The Holy Spirit is one of the things that separates Christianity from other religions. We have the Spirit of God residing in us. We can feel the Spirit inside of us. It leads and guides us unto righteousness, it teaches us, it comforts us, it empowers us in the word, it empowers us to live a Christian life, it empowers our testimony and our Christian witness, and it bears witness with our spirit that we are children of God. If we try to do these things in our own strength, we will fail,; but through the power of the Holy Spirit and Jesus, we are more than conquerors. We can do all things through Christ.

Jesus Christ and the Holy Spirit is the empowerment of a Christian.

When you accept Jesus during the Tribulation, the Holy Spirit will empower you to: (1) die as a witness for Jesus or

(2) survive the Tribulation and come into the thousand-year reign as a living flesh-and-blood person. Let us discuss both possibilities.

After the antichrist or the beast is established, he will begin to decree many laws. Daniel 7:25 says, "He shall speak pompous words against the most high and shall intend to change time and laws." Daniel 11:36 says, "He shall magnify himself above every god and speak blasphemies against the God of Gods, and shall prosper until the wrath (Tribulation) has been accomplished."

Those who want to make heaven their home must avoid following this world leader, even if the government of your country supports him. This can be done and you will be deemed righteous at the judgment of the nations. Your nation's leaders will be deemed unrighteous at that time.

By believing in Jesus and not following the antichrist, you will have positioned yourself to be with the "sheep" at the judgment of the nations. Zechariah 2:11 tells us, "Many nations shall be joined to the Lord in that day, and they will become my people. I will dwell in your midst that you may know that I am the Lord." We will surely know that Jesus is Lord. He will be living and reigning right here on earth.

At the midpoint of the Tribulation, the world ruler will issue two decrees that you must not obey under any circumstance. They are: worship the world ruler and take a number to buy and sell. Revelation 13:15–18 tells us:

> He was granted power to give breath to the image of the beast. That the beast should both speak and cause as many as would not worship the image of the beast to be killed.
>
> And he caused all, both small and great, rich and poor, free and slave, to receive a mark on their right hand or in their forehead, that no one may buy or sell except the one who has the mark of the beast, or the number of his name. Here is wisdom. Let him who has understanding calculate the number of the beast, for it is the number of a man: His number is six hundred, three score, and six.

Reading this number as 666 is meaningless, and I will address that later in this chapter. The image of the beast has breath, can speak, and causes people to be put to death. This is not just an animated act of talking like we see in museums. This image can discern who is worshiping and who is not.

Everyone is ordered to worship the beast and to receive the number. It's gut check time on earth! Millions will disobey and become outlaws. Jesus warns us:

> You will be brought before governors and kings for my sake, as a testimony to them and to the gentiles. But when they deliver you up, do not worry about how or what you should speak, for it will be given you in that hour what you should speak; for it is not you who speak, but the spirit of your Father

> who speaks in you. Now brother will deliver brother to death, and a father his child; and children will rise up against parents and cause them to be put to death. And you will be hated by all for my name's sake. But he who endures to the end will be saved.

You will be brought before governors and kings as a testimony for Jesus. Do not premeditate your answers. That will cause failure. The Holy Spirit will give you the answers to their questions, and it will be a great witness of Jesus to a lost world.

How did you get turned in to the authorities and delivered "up" to governors and kings? Most likely by one of your family members that did take the number. Verse 21 says, "Brother will deliver brother to death and a father will deliver his child to death." Children will cause their parents to be put to death. These Scriptures can only be fulfilled during the Tribulation. The totalitarian decrees issued by the antichrist will cause this breakdown of common morals and human decency. It is now dog-eat-dog and every man for himself. There will be great pressure on the people who take the number to turn in people who do not take the number. There may even be a reward for the information. Why is it family members are doing this? Simply put, they are the ones who know where you are. It should be noted that the children mentioned here are full-grown adults.

This statement is hurtful to think about but you must be aware of this fact. If you do not take the number, you cannot trust anyone who did take the number, not even your own children or your parents or your brothers or sisters. They cannot and will not cover for you. They will deliver you up to death. You will need to hide from everyone who knows you. You will be *hated* by all, "but he who endures to the end shall be saved." Being permanently separated from children or parents may be the hardest part of the Tribulation. There will be great turmoil on earth. To face execution and get out of the madness may come as a great relief. The ones who are executed for their testimony of Jesus now have victory over Satan.

Moving ahead, Revelation 14:9–11 warns:

> If anyone worships the beast and his image and receives his mark on his forehead or in his hand, he shall also drink of the wine of the wrath of God, which is poured out full strength into the cup of his indignation. And he shall be tormented with fire and brimstone in the presence of the Holy Angels and in the presence of the Lamb. And the smoke of their torment ascends forever and ever; and they have no rest day or night who worship the beast or his image, and whoever receives the mark of his name.

Can you make it without buying or selling? It will be hard and you will have to be resourceful, but it can be done. Trust in Jesus, and he will see you through.

You can be saved during the Tribulation. Believe in and confess Jesus Christ as the Son of God. Maintain your testimony to the end. Do not worship the beast or his image. Do not take the number to buy or sell. If you are caught and accused of being a Christian, plead guilty. You will lose your life but will gain eternal life with the Lord.

You will also reign with Christ during the thousand-year reign. Revelation 20:4–6 says,

> I saw the souls of those who were beheaded for their witness to Jesus and for the word of God, who had not worshiped the beast or his image, and had not received his mark on their forehead or in their hands. And they lived and reigned with Christ for one thousand years. But the rest of the dead (unrighteous dead) did not live again until the one thousand years were finished.
>
> This is the first resurrection. Blessed and holy is he who has part in the first resurrection. Over such, the second death (hell) has no power, but they shall be priests of God and of Christ, and shall reign with him a thousand years.

Those who are beheaded because of their Christian stand will be included with the raptured church as the first resurrection. They will reign with Christ as kings and priests. We infer from this that the end of the Tribulation is also the end of the church age. People will be saved throughout the Tribulation and until its end.

I will regress here and talk about the number that was touched on earlier. The original text shows the number like this: six hundred, threescore, and six. Somewhere in the last thirty to forty years, the new versions shortened this to 666. Most changes in the modern versions aren't of much significance, but this one has caused misunderstanding of how the world numbering system will be implemented.

Let's look at the number in more detail. The Bible tells us that all will be ordered to receive this number. Why? The world will be experiencing severe economic problems at this time, and giving everyone a number in order to buy and sell will look like a possible solution. It will also be put forth as the solution to several periphery problems such as robberies, counterfeiting, and muggings. There will be no money to counterfeit and nothing to rob. We are already doing things that prepare us to receive this number. How efficient is this? Your numbered account is automatically credited with your earnings. The government takes a known percentage, and ta-da, no more taxes to file.

Your account is automatically debited when you buy something, and this is done by passing your hand in front of a scanner. It will automatically credit the store's account and automatically track store inventory. The store's system would automatically reorder at the time it was keyed to do so. We are already doing these things except for going cashless and putting the number in our hand or forehead. The number is now in our pocket or purse, and we have to fumble around for it.

The number that goes in our hand or forehead will most likely be on a small computer chip. It will likely contain a GPS or global positioning system to assist in finding lost persons, abducted children, or criminals. Remember, it will also show where *you* are. We already use these chips on our pets. This will cause people to feel more secure, and the idea will be well received. Your number will be more important than your name. Besides the number that is unique to you, it may contain other pertinent data such as medical history. All of this can be accessed by scanning your hand.

Do not take this number! After taking or rejecting the number, everyone is committed one way or the other, and do remember, those who take it are "tormented with fire and brimstone forever and ever, and have no rest day or night." By refusing this number, you will be causing problems with the full implementation of the system. You will be executed if you are caught. This will all go down at the midpoint of the Tribulation. If you refuse the number, you will have to survive for three and a half years without the ability to buy or sell. It will be very helpful to live in a rural area. You will also have to evade the authorities who may be looking for those who refuse the number. They will not be able to track you electronically if you did not take the number.

There will be great pressure put on everyone to take the number and become part of the world economic system. It will be considered the patriotic thing to do as the entire world will be attempting to address severe economic problems.

The world's financial status right now (2012) is on very "thin ice." Many of the world's banks are technically bankrupt, and many nations are on the verge of economic chaos or collapse.

As of now (2012), the United States is reportedly sixteen trillion dollars in debt with no way in sight to become financially solvent. It matters not if the president is a Democrat or Republican. We are borrowing money to make payments on borrowed money and then are only able to pay the interest. If this continues, the collapse of the world monetary system is inevitable. I have never been pessimistic, but it seems that we are headed down a slippery financial slope that cannot be reversed. The world will try to correct this with a new way to "buy and sell."

Our current world leaders are already trying to formulate a "new world economic order." As the nations of the world pull together to attempt to solve this monetary crisis, they are already discussing a "one world currency" and even a "one world government." The mentality is that we are all in this thing together. All of this is conditioning us for the government of the antichrist. It will all seem logical and desirable, and most people will cooperate fully with the new world leader. They will perceive, and rightly so, that everyone is on this "sinking ship" and that everyone must help "right the boat".

Now, back to the number. According to the Bible, it is in the same format as our social security number. The number listed is 600-60-6, and the verse tells us that it is the number of the antichrist himself. He will be in the system also and will lead the way with this number.

The number 6 denotes military leadership. The call sign ending with 6 always denotes the commander of any given military unit.

If the number happens to be your social security number, you can still reject it. You have not taken the number until they implant it in your hand or forehead. It will probably be a similar grouping of numbers generated out of the computer storage banks. That would be easier than inputting everyone's social security number into the world computer.

The consensus opinion that I have heard is that everyone will have the number 666 in their hand or forehead. What will that accomplish? The world will need a high-tech solution in a high-tech society. Everything a person needs will be in a small chip in the back of their hand. Everyone's number will be different just as credit card numbers are different. The number will identify you and you only.

Do you want victory? Revelation 15:2 tells us,

> I saw as it were a sea of glass mingled with fire: and them that had gotten victory over the beast, and over his image, and over his mark, and over the number of his name, standing on the sea of glass, having harps of God.

I will shout it from the rooftop, "Don't take the number to buy or sell!"

If you miss the Rapture of the church, you can still be saved, even under the brutal conditions of the Tribulation. If you worship the beast or take the number, you cannot be saved. Everyone who worships the beast or takes the number will end up in hell. Here is how it plays out: The followers of the antichrist who die during the Tribulation, and there will be hundreds of millions, will go to hell. Those who are following the antichrist at the battle of Armageddon will all be slain and go to hell. The antichrist or beast and the false prophet who assisted him will be cast alive into the lake of fire burning with brimstone. There will be additional millions of antichrist supporters throughout the earth, and they will be judged at the judgment of the nations and banished into everlasting fire. All followers of the antichrist are now in hell, and the antichrist himself has been cast into the lake of fire. The lake of fire is not hell but is a final place of torment that the Lord has created. Hell will eventually be cast into the lake of fire. It is interesting to note that the beast and the false prophet will occupy this lake of fire by themselves for one thousand years.

In 2 Thessalonians 1:6–10, it describes Jesus's second coming and the battle of Armageddon. Follow closely.

> Since it is a righteous thing with God to *repay* with Tribulation those who trouble you, and to give you who are troubled rest with us when the Lord Jesus is revealed from heaven, with his mighty angels, in flaming fire taking vengeance on those who do not

1000 Years of Perfect Justice | 53

> know God, and on those who do not obey the gospel of our Lord Jesus Christ. These shall be punished with everlasting destruction from the presence of our Lord and from the glory of his power, when he comes in that day, to be glorified in his saints and to be admired among all those who believe, because our testimony among you was believed.

The flaming fire that Jesus takes vengeance with is not the destruction of the earth with fire as some believe. He takes vengeance on those who do not know God when he cast the beast and the false prophet into the lake of fire and slays the armies that followed them. These followers also go to hell. Directly after the battle of Armageddon, Jesus then assembles all the people left in the world and judges them. He tells the wicked, "Depart from me you cursed, into the everlasting fire prepared for the devil and his angels." With that, we see that every person who followed the antichrist has ended up in hell. They traded three and a half years of being able to buy and sell for eternal damnation. We will see in the next chapter that those three and a half years were total misery.

We need to tie up a couple of loose ends before we continue. Hell is located in the inner parts of earth. We, on the surface, are not very far from hell. The people in hell will stay there until the great white throne judgment. That occurs after the thousand-year reign has ended. Hell will then be emptied and everyone judged. They will then be cast into the lake of fire.

Satan will be held in the bottomless pit during the thousand-year reign. Revelation 20:1–3 says:

> I saw an Angel having the key to the bottomless pit and a great chain in his hand. He laid hold of the Devil, who is Satan, and bound him for one thousand years; and he cast him into the bottomless pit, so that he should deceive the nations no more until the one thousand years were finished.

Matthew 25:31–34 and 41 tells us:

> When the Son of Man comes in his glory and all the Holy Angels with him, then he will sit on the Throne of his glory. (The rebuilt Temple in Jerusalem) All nations will be gathered before him and he will separate them one from another, as a shepherd divides his sheep from his goats.

The criteria for sheep are:

1. Did not worship the beast or take the number.
2. Did not support your nation if they supported the antichrist.
3. Did nothing to harm Israel but supported Israel as best you could.
4. Did keep your trust in Jesus until his second coming.

The criteria for the goats is exactly opposite of the sheep, but I will list them anyway:

1. Did take the number and did worship the beast.
2. Did support your nation in their support of the antichrist.
3. Did not care about the sufferings of Israel.
4. Did not trust in Jesus but rather cursed and blasphemed.

These people will make all sorts of claims to Jesus, but it will be out of desperation. They will know that they are lying and that Jesus knows they are lying.

Continuing with the Scripture, "And he will set the sheep on his right hand but the goats on the left. Then the King will say to those on his right hand, 'Come, you blessed of my Father, inherit the kingdom prepared for you from the foundation of the world.'" We have already noted that Jesus tells the goats "Depart from me you cursed, into the everlasting fire prepared for the Devil and his angels."

You sometimes hear the judgment of the nations preached as the great white throne judgment. This is probably because you hear the same judgments pronounced, but the difference is that Jesus is pronouncing to living people to "depart into everlasting fire prepared for the Devil and his angels." Everyone at the white throne judgment will have been brought up from the dead. Some will have been dead for thousands of years. All of the unrighteous dead will be brought out of hell, judged, and cast into the lake of fire.

This was described by Jesus as outer darkness. Matthew 8:11–12 says, "I say to you that many will sit down with Abraham, Isaac, and Jacob in the kingdom of heaven. But the sons of the kingdom will be cast into outer darkness. There will be weeping and gnashing of teeth."

Only the righteous are left on earth for the thousand-year reign. Jesus has subdued all enemies and the people left on earth will worship and serve him. If you survive the Tribulation believing in Jesus, you will be saved and have eternal life with Jesus. If you are judged as one of the "sheep," you will go through the thousand-year reign as a flesh-and-blood person. Are you ready to live for a one thousand years? You will also comingle with the glorified saints.

Jesus said that for the elects' sake, the days of the Tribulation are shortened. He also said that unless those days were shortened, no flesh would be saved. The elect spoken of is the nation of Israel. Zechariah 13:8–9 says,

> And it shall come to pass in all the land, says the Lord, that two-thirds in it shall be cut off and die, but one-third shall be left. I will bring the one-third through the fire, I will refine them as silver is refined, and test them as gold is tested. They shall call on my name and I shall answer them. I will say this is my people, and EACH ONE will say, the Lord is my God.

All followers of Jesus that survive the Tribulation are blessed, but Israel is the elect. They will turn to Jesus at the battle of Armageddon.

The righteous that survive the Tribulation will probably be the young, strong, and resourceful. The ones who are healthy and can fend for themselves. They will not need doctors or medicines. They will be able to survive under harsh conditions and will not have to have regular or balanced meals. They will be able to eat whatever is available, whenever it is available. These are the ones that will begin to repopulate the earth during the thousand-year reign.

Do not "bet the farm" on evading the antichrist and surviving the Tribulation. It will be possible, and millions will survive. Millions of others will die at the hands of the beast. The people with the best chance of avoiding or evading the world leader's edicts will be those farthest removed from the Middle East, the Far East, and Europe.

This will include all of the southern hemisphere, the United States, and Canada. His attempt to rule the world will be enforced most intensely in the Middle East and Europe.

As you get farther from the seat of power, there will be less ability to control the populace. This should also hold true if your nation is supportive of the world policy. Rural people should fare better than city people due to less availability. Not being able to buy or sell will be a major problem for persons in cities and industrialized nations. It may not be much of a problem for less affluent or third world countries. There are millions of people in third world countries and in many South American countries that live on their own subsistence. They barter for other items as necessary. You only have to hold out for three and a half years. It will be possible to survive for that long, but wouldn't it be better to "love his appearing" and take the first flight out with the raptured church!

Here's a brief recap: if you miss the Rapture, and many will, even church members, you can still be saved.

Hold fast your testimony until the end. That is, the end of your life or the end of the Tribulation. Do not obey the decrees of the world leader. You will be in survival mode for three and a half years. You will not live well, but all you have to do is *survive*. There is a great day coming for you, and that day will be covered in chapter 7.

Jesus exhorts us in Luke 21:36 to "Watch therefore, and pray always that you may be counted worthy to escape all those things that will come to pass, and to stand before the Son of Man." Jesus then promises the church in Revelation 3:10, "Because you have kept my command to *persevere*, I also will keep you from the hour of trial which will come upon the whole world, to test those who dwell on earth."

Are you praying that you be found worthy to "escape all those things"?" We can escape "those things," and we are worthy through faith in Jesus Christ. Jesus then promises that if we "persevere," or keep our trust in him, he will keep us from that hour. Jesus can come at any time.

Are you ready? This chapter is for someone out there.

THE TRIBULATION: PART 1

ISRAEL

He shall confirm a covenant with many for one week.

Daniel 9:27

How will we know when the Tribulation begins? Daniel 9:27 tells us, "Then he shall confirm a covenant with many for one week, but in the middle of the week he shall bring an end to sacrifice and offering." He, in this verse, is the antichrist. The week represents seven years, rather than seven days. The covenant will be a peace treaty with Israel, which will be limited to a seven-year time frame.

It will probably be necessary to put this time limit on the treaty in order for the Arab nations to go along with it. Note that it will be confirmed by "many."

We are then told that in the middle of the week, not three and a half days but three and a half years, that he, the antichrist, shall bring an end to sacrifice and offering. Three and a half years is the midpoint of the Tribulation and is the same point that the antichrist decrees that everyone must worship him or his image and take the number in order to buy or sell. So we will know for sure when the midpoint is, but how will we know when the Tribulation begins?

It will simply be when the seven-year peace treaty with Israel is signed and ratified by all the nations concerned.

There will probably be a lot of publicity and fanfare surrounding this event and the people of the world will be relieved that Israel and her enemies have finally made peace. Oddly enough, the Israelis themselves will be deceived into thinking that this is a lasting peace. There are some who will think that Israel will initially believe the antichrist to be the messiah. I don't see how they could be that deceived, but it may happen that way.

There is nothing in the Scriptures to indicate exactly when this peace treaty is agreed to, so it could be immediately prior to the Rapture or sometime after the Rapture. But do know this: if the church is still here when the seven-year peace treaty is signed, our deliverance is at hand!

The church will not suffer any part of the Tribulation.

Jesus promised us that he would "keep us from the hour of trial which will come upon the whole world, to test those who dwell on earth." Christians may see the peace treaty signed and agreed to, but Christians will not suffer any adverse effects of the Tribulation. The church will be caught away, and then the troubles will begin.

What is the purpose of the Tribulation? There are two main reasons documented in the Scriptures. Remember that God is in total control of everything that is happening. This is the way that he chooses to bring this age to conclusion. The first reason for the Tribulation is to bring a final testing and chastisement on the nation and people of Israel.

The second reason is to deal with Satan and his followers who brazenly oppose God. We will discuss Israel first.

Ezekiel 36:16–19, 22, 23 says:

> Moreover the word of the Lord came to me, saying: Son of Man, when the house of Israel dwelt in their own land, they defiled it by their own ways and deeds; To me their way was like the uncleanness of a woman in her customary impurity. Therefore I poured out my fury on them for the blood they had shed on the land, and for their idols with which they defiled it. So I scattered them among the nations and they were dispersed throughout the countries. Therefore say to the house of Israel, thus says the Lord God: I do not do this for your sake, house of Israel, but for my Holy name's sake, which you have profaned among the nations wherever you went. And will sanctify my great name, which has been profaned among the nations, which you have profaned in their midst; and the nations will know that I am the Lord, says the Lord God, when I am hallowed in you before their eyes.

The Lord described Israel's sin as being like a woman's menstrual cycle. The Lord poured out his fury and scattered them among the nations of the world. The final dispersion occurred in the first century when the Romans destroyed Jerusalem and the temple in AD 70. Jews were scattered all over the world, but several things should be noted.

1. For almost two thousand years, although scattered worldwide, Israelites have maintained their national identity, they continue Jewish customs and traditions, such as Passover, and they observe the law, even without a temple or central place of worship.
2. Wherever they went, some excelled and some did not, many were subjected to poverty, and almost all were persecuted just for being Jewish. The most extreme case of persecution was the Holocaust. Between six to eight million Jews, only God knows the exact number, were rounded up by Hitler's Nazi Germany, gassed to death, and then cremated. Jews have suffered more persecution than any other race of people. I know that is debatable, but again, just consider the Holocaust.

    It wasn't that many years ago that many misconceptions existed in America. I was warned as a teenager in the 1950's that the Jews were trying to "take over the world." When I became an adult in the 1960's, many Americans believed that twelve Jews met every Monday in Chicago and decided everything of importance for our nation, even who would be president.

They supposedly controlled all the banks and all of the money. The Jewish people have suffered the effects of this type of hysteria down through the ages. This has been allowed by God, but do remember, some of us have played a part in this persecution.

3. They have retained God's promise of a messiah—a day that will bring them all back to Israel to live in peace and safety. Will the little country hold all of them? Yes! In Genesis 15:18, God made a covenant with Abraham, saying, "To your descendants I have given this land, from the river of Egypt to the great river, the river Euphrates." Looking at a map, we see that from the Nile River to the Euphrates River it takes in the eastern half of Egypt, all of Jordan, Syria, Lebanon, the northern half of Saudi Arabia, the western half of Iraq, and of course, Israel. We will see later that all of this land will become like the garden of Eden during the thousand-year reign. In Genesis 17:18–19, God specifies that this covenant is absolutely through Isaac, not Ishmael, and to his Jewish descendants.

And Abraham said to God, Oh, that Ishmael might live before you!" Then God said, "No, Sarah your wife shall bear you a son, and you shall call his name Isaac; I will establish my covenant with him for an everlasting covenant, and with his descendants after him."

Jesus is very close to coming back to set up his kingdom on earth, but there will be seven years of Tribulation before this happens. In Daniel 10:14, the angel Gabriel says to Daniel, "Now I have come to make you understand what will happen to 'your people' in the latter days, for the vision refers to many days yet to come."

"Your people" (Daniel's people) are the Jewish people, and the Jewish people are the ones referred to as "saints," or "holy people" in all of the end of the age Scriptures.

The angel Gabriel plainly says to Daniel, "This is what will happen to 'your people.'" When the antichrist violates his covenant with Israel at the midpoint of the Tribulation, he will do more than decree himself to be God and to be worshiped and more than implement a worldwide economic system. He will also declare war on Israel with the intent of "wiping them off the map" and ensuring that they "no longer exist as a people." Do these phrases sound familiar? They should. They are being said on television almost daily by many Arab leaders of the world. Daniel 8:23–24 says:

> And in the latter time of their kingdom, when transgressors have reached their fullness, a king shall arise, having fierce features, who understands sinister schemes. His power shall be mighty, but not by his own power; he shall destroy fearfully, and shall prosper and thrive; he shall destroy the mighty and also the Holy people.

In this verse, we find him destroying the "holy people" (Israel). Daniel 12:7 says, "When the power of the *holy people* has been completely shattered, all these things shall be finished." Completely shattered, Israel will have no power of her own and will be crying out for God to save her people. Revelation 13:6–7 says, "Then he opened his mouth in blasphemy against God, to blaspheme his name, his tabernacle, and those who dwell in heaven. And it was granted to him to make war with the saints and to overcome them."

Again, saints and holy people refer to Israel. We have previously noted that two-thirds of Israel will be cut off and die, but one-third will survive. God will bring this one-third through the fire and adversity of the tribulation.

He will refine them like gold and make them pure. They will call on his name, and God will answer them. The Lord will declare that "this, Israel, is my people." Every Israelite will gladly declare, "The Lord is my god!"

Two-thirds will die and one-third will survive. It is interesting to note that a recent poll showed that two-thirds of the Jews in Israel did not believe in God and that one-third did believe in God. If these poll numbers are correct, they agree exactly with Ezekiel's words penned thousands of years ago. The only thing that will save Israel at the battle of Armageddon is their dependence on God. It makes sense to me that the two-thirds who will die are those who do not trust in God. The one-third who will survive and are rescued by Jesus are those who do trust in God. It will be like the days of old for Israel. When they had no hope, they would earnestly cry out to God, and he would come to their rescue, destroy their enemies, and restore them to fellowship. Zechariah 12:10 tells us:

> I will pour on the house of David and on the inhabitants of Jerusalem the spirit of grace and supplication; Then they will look on me whom they pierced; They will mourn for him as one mourns for his only son, and grieve for him as one grieves for a firstborn.

What is this saying? The Jewish people will recognize Jesus as the Messiah that their forefathers crucified two thousand years ago. They will mourn and grieve and be sorrowful that they have missed God all these years. They will believe in Jesus. They do not believe in Jesus at this time. They will repent of their sins, especially the sin of unbelief. These verses are in the Jewish Holy Scripture and have been available to the Jewish people since Zechariah penned them. That was about five hundred years before Christ was born. Jesus accused the Jews of slaying Zechariah between the altar and the temple. It may have been for this very prophecy.

The nation of Israel will refuse to worship the beast or his image. The world ruler will use this as an excuse to "wipe them off the earth." That was his agenda all along.

Israel will be in constant war during the last three and a half years of the Tribulation. They will be facing what looks like certain annihilation. Jesus then comes and destroys their enemies. Their great suffering has ended. Israel will become the greatest nation on earth. That will be covered in chapter 7.

Ezekiel 39:21–29 summarizes Israel's situation thusly:

> I will set my glory among the nations; all the nations shall see my judgment which I have executed, and my hand which I have laid on them. So the house of Israel shall know that I am the Lord their God from that day forward.
>
> The Gentiles shall know that the house of Israel went into captivity for their iniquity; because they were unfaithful to me, therefore I hid my face from them. I gave them into the hand of their enemies, and they all fell by the sword. According to their uncleanness and according to their transgressions I have dealt with them and hidden my face from them. Therefore thus says the Lord God. Now I will bring back the captives of Jacob and have mercy on the whole house of Israel.
>
> When I have brought them back from the peoples and gathered them out of their enemies lands, and am hallowed in them in the sight of many nations, then they shall know that I am the Lord their God who sent them into captivity among the nations, but also brought them back to their own

> land, and left none of them captive any longer. And I will not hide my face from them anymore; for I shall have poured out my spirit on the house of Israel, says the Lord God.

We get several things from these Scriptures. The Gentiles *shall know* that Israel went into captivity for their iniquity. They are still God's chosen people, but he is chastening them for their sins and unfaithfulness.

We know that whom the Lord loves, he chastens. God dealt with them according to their transgressions. What did this severe chastening accomplish? "They shall know that I am the Lord their God!" Israel will know that God is real and so will all the people of the earth. Now, we live by faith, and God blesses those who believe without seeing.

The day is coming, and soon, I believe, when our faith will become reality. Jesus will live with us, and everyone will know the Lord!

Jeremiah 30:7 provides us this insight: "Alas! for that day is great, so that none is like it; and it is the time of Jacob's troubles, but he shall be saved out of it."

The time of Jacob's trouble is between God and his people, Israel. It may not seem fair to us, but remember, God is in complete control. He is chastening Israel for their ultimate benefit. He will do the same for us. Accept God's chastening, and be thankful for it. Grow as a Christian and benefit from it. Grow closer to God and depend on him more because of it. When Jesus comes in power and great glory, the time of Jacob's troubles will be over. It will be glorious during the thousand-year reign. We will get into that in chapter 7.

I hope that this is making more sense now. God has dealt and is dealing with his people Israel. He will chasten them and bring them through the fire. He will have a tested people that he will save and restore. They will then serve him fully and faithfully as was intended from the beginning.

He will be their God and say, "They are my people." They will say joyfully, "The Lord is my God!" The remnant of Israel along with the church will serve Jesus as kings and priests for one thousand years.

THE TRIBULATION: PART 2

THE ANTICHRIST

Then there shall be great tribulation, such as has not been since the world began.

Matthew 24:21

Not to be tedious, but let's do a brief recap to transition into the next phase of the Tribulation.

The antichrist has risen to power. He signs a seven-year peace treaty with Israel and then violates it at the midpoint (three and a half years). He outlaws all worship except of himself or his image. He establishes a worldwide system to buy and sell. He makes war against the saints and prevails. He speaks pompous words against the Most High. He persecutes the saints of the Most High. The saints shall be given into his hand for three and a half years, and he will intend to change times and laws. He takes away the daily sacrifice and tramples the sanctuary underfoot. He destroys the holy people.

It appears that everything is "pie peachy pie pie," to quote from an old song, for the antichrist but "not so fast."

Daniel 7:23 says simply, "And the Ancient of days (God) came and a judgment was made in favor of the saints of the most high, and the time came for the saints to possess the kingdom." This verse sounds calm and sedate, but God decreed it and it is packed with power.

During the last three and a half years of the Tribulation, it will look like the good guys are losing by the blowout rule, but God is meting out punishment upon the wicked also. This is one last effort to get those who will to repent and to punish those who will not repent. God accomplishes this with three separate judgments. They are the seal judgments, the trumpet judgments, and the bowl judgments. The only thing we need to see by these judgments is how devastated the earth becomes and how terrible life is on earth. I will summarize each one as briefly as possible.

THE SEAL JUDGMENTS

The first seal describes a rider on a white horse.

He has a bow and goes forth to conquer. The white horse indicates that he will appear to be peaceful. The bow represents a lesser weapon than swords or spears. He will use force sparingly at this time. This rider represents the antichrist, and his initial alliances will be accomplished by diplomacy. Things seem fairly normal at this time.

The second seal describes a rider on a red horse. He has a great sword and begins to make war against the nations. The nations that allied with the antichrist are now fighting those nations that are holding out. This war causes massive death, but it is only the beginning.

The third seal describes a black horse. The rider has a set of scales in his hand. The black horse represents famine throughout the earth. The scales represent that food is almost nonexistent and has to be measured out very carefully. A quart of wheat cost a denarius. This is super inflation as a denarius equaled a days pay in the first century AD. This came about because of the war that was waged with the red horse. I also suspect ineptitude and mismanagement on the part of the world leader. God is in control, and the "noose" is being tightened.

The fourth seal describes a pale horse, which represents death. The rider of this horse is called Death. Hell follows this horse, and a fourth of the earth is slain.

Many of these deaths were caused by famine and, interestingly, by the animals of the earth.

The fourth part of the earth could be 25 percent of the entire earth. It could be a fourth of the earth in one area such as the Middle East, Europe, or Africa. One-fourth of the earth's population, at this time, will equal about one billion people. We have worldwide war, no food supply to count on, and people are starving and being killed by lions, tigers, and other large animals. Earth is now a terrible place to live in. Although hell followed this horse, we cannot assume that no Christians were killed. The fifth seal indicates otherwise.

The animals of the earth get involved in this killing.

I once thought that there were no animals in America that could kill a person. I was wrong. Counting zoos, circuses, game preserves, and here's the biggie: private citizens who keep large cats, there are over five thousand lions, tigers, and other large cats in America. According to a recent TV documentary, there are more large cats caged in America than are in the wild in Africa.

I saw a televised news story about a woman who had 147 big cats, mostly lions, in fourteen-foot chain-link fencing.

She said she had to scrounge a ton of meat per day to feed them. When asked why she did it, she said she didn't know. It just seemed like something someone needed to do in order to help the animals. When asked what she would do if she could no longer feed them, she replied, "I would just open the gates and let them go". Its scary to think about. Five thousand big cats in America can be let go or escape on their own. Is the day coming when they will be loosed for the purpose of killing human beings? Big cats in the wild have some fear of humans, but these have been raised and fed by humans. They will have no fear of us. To be killed by a lion or tiger would be a horrible way to die, but the stage is set right here in America.

The fifth seal describes the souls of all those who were slain during the Tribulation. They were slain because they stood for Jesus and would not recant their testimony.

By allowing themselves to be beheaded, they have gotten victory over the beast. This seal indicates that multitudes of their brethren and fellow servants will give their life by the end of the Tribulation. Jesus said that whoever saved his life would lose it, but whoever loses his life would save it. This teaching will certainly apply during the Tribulation. Again, if you find yourself in the Tribulation, maintain your belief in Jesus and have this testimony to the end. Your reward will be great in heaven. We overcome Satan by the blood of the Lamb and the word of our testimony. These people maintained their testimony of Jesus and allowed themselves to be executed rather than worship the beast or take the number to buy and sell.

It should be noted that first-century Christians also suffered execution by the Roman government. They were given the option of recanting Jesus or execution. They were beheaded. They were fed to lions in the coliseum as thousands watched the "sport".

They were burned at the stake. The list could go on.

It appears that beheading will be the preferred method used during the Tribulation. Mankind has not progressed much in our dealings with each other in the last two thousand years.

We will do much better in the next one thousand years. I promise!

By allowing themselves to be executed, these people overcome Satan and enter into eternal life. They did not "love their life" but loved eternal life with Jesus. Great is their reward for this brave act. God's grace will be sufficient for all those who take that stand in that day.

Make up your mind, refuse to recant, and relax. You will be with Jesus in a matter of seconds.

The second thing we see is that additional people, possibly millions, will be slain throughout the Tribulation.

Revelation 7:9, 14 tells us of a great multitude that no man could number. One of the elders ask, "Who are these and where did they come from?" He was answered in verse 14, "These are the ones who come out of great Tribulation, and washed their robes and made them white in the blood of the Lamb."

Those slain during the Tribulation, for their testimony of Jesus, will return with Jesus for the thousand-year reign.

The sixth seal describes horrific events that will look like natural disasters but will be sent straight from God. There will be a great earthquake, the sun will become black, and the moon like blood. The stars will fall to earth. The sky will recede like a scroll when it is rolled up. Every mountain and island will be moved out of its place. Men of all social status will try to hide from the great wrath of God. They will be crying out for the rocks to fall on them.

They sense that they are doomed, but with all of this, wicked men will not repent. They curse God for these plagues.

Can you imagine how strange this will look? The sun will be black or appear that way, the moon will be red like blood, and the stars will fall to earth. Most of the stars will probably burn up, but lots of them will make it to earth.

They will probably range from gravel-size up to house-size and larger. Most stars are much larger than earth. They will need to burn to a manageable size prior to impact.

The earth is now in what looks like an empty void. There is no sky. There are no stars except the ones you are tripping over. You cannot see the sun, and the moon is red like blood. This will be overwhelming to people on earth.

Man's reaction to these events is to try to hide from God. Man has been trying to hide from God ever since Adam and Eve attempted it in the garden of Eden. These wicked men recognize both God and Jesus. They cry out to the rocks, "Hide us from him who sits on the throne and from the wrath of the Lamb." The ultimate act of futility is asking the rocks to hide you from God. More of God's wrath will be poured out as we continue with the judgments. Men will continue to harden themselves, blaspheme God, and refuse to repent. Again, those who worshiped the beast or took the number cannot receive forgiveness. They are doomed.

The seventh seal describes seven angels standing before God. They are given seven trumpets that will be sounded for the next round of judgments. Another angel was given much incense to offer with the prayers of the saints. He offered it upon the golden altar before the throne of God. The smoke of the incense and the prayers of the saints ascend to God. The angel then takes fire from the altar and throws it to earth. The seven angels with the seven trumpets now prepare to sound.

We do want to note here that our prayers, every prayer ever prayed by every saint, gets mixed with incense and fire from the altar of God. We have long since forgotten most of our prayers. We may remember the "big" ones, but God has all of them. When they are offered with incense to God, he breathes them in as a sweet-smelling savor.

That makes me want to pray more. I hope you will also.

THE TRUMPET JUDGMENTS

The first trumpet describes hail and fire, mingled with blood, being thrown to earth. This causes a third of the trees and all green grass to be burned up. The earth was looking very bleak at the end of the seal judgments, and now the earth's surface is blackened from all the green grass burning up. It's a horror story. Try to keep up with these events. The earth will be devastated but when Jesus reigns for a thousand years, he will cause this same earth to be like "the garden of Eden".

The second trumpet describes a great mountain, burning with fire, being thrown into the sea. A third of the sea becomes blood, a third of the creatures in the sea die, and a third of the ships were destroyed. The sea becomes blood, not just a red color, but blood. A third of the sea life dies, and a third of the ships are destroyed. The seas are now a frightful place to be. Thousands of people perish at sea when those ships are destroyed.

The third trumpet describes a great star falling from heaven, burning like a torch. It fell on a third of the rivers and the springs of water. Many men die because of the bitter water. This is another event that could cause great loss of life. Everyone has to drink water.

The fourth trumpet describes a third of the sun and a third of the moon being struck, so that a third of them were darkened and a third of the day did not shine and likewise the night.

The sun, moon, and stars are smitten. At this point, great terror and dread must be overcoming the wicked inhabitants of earth. However, those maintaining their belief and testimony of Jesus have to be encouraged by these events. Jesus tells us in Luke 21:25–28:

> Then there will be signs in the Sun, in the Moon, and in the stars; and on earth distress of nations, with perplexity, the sea and the waves roaring; mens hearts failing them from fear and expectation of those things which are coming on the earth, for the powers of the heaven will be shaken.

Verse 28 then says, "When these things begin to happen, look up and lift up your heads, because your redemption draws near!" Verse 27 then says that "They will see the Son of Man coming with power and great glory." Lift up your heads! The good guys are about to win! (PS: we have already read the book and know how it ends!) Let me note "the sea and waves roaring." Tsunamis are a new thing on earth. I don't recall them occurring more than ten to fifteen years ago, so I'm going to say the tsunamis we have seen lately, Japan being the latest, is a lead in to the end of the age. It's just one more thing that helps us "see the day approaching."

The fifth trumpet describes the bottomless pit being opened. The sun and the air are darkened because of the smoke that came out of the pit. Then locusts come out of the pit with the command to harm only the men who did not have the seal of God on their foreheads. These locusts can only harm the followers of the antichrist. They could not kill them but were authorized to torment them for five months. Their sting is like the sting of a scorpion. The misery will be so bad that men will desire to die but cannot. This shows us that God is in total control. God has sent these things to torment wicked men, and he will not let them die until they have suffered to the maximum. Men will evidently attempt to commit suicide and not be successful. That seems strange to us, but the word of God says that it is appointed once for man to die. There are many causes of death, but this is the "reason" we die. God said that it is appointed for us.

These locust are shaped like horses, have faces like men, hair like a woman's, teeth like lions, breastplates like iron, wings to fly, tails like scorpions, with the sting in their tails.

Imagine, if you can, having to confront these "things" every day. You must avoid their sting or suffer terrible agony. Conditions are already horrible on earth, and these things will double or triple the misery. They may be able to break into houses. It will be a real, live, horror story that the followers of the antichrist will have to endure.

The sixth trumpet describes four angels that are bound at the great river Euphrates. They have been prepared for a specific hour, day, month, and year. They are released and kill a third of mankind. Earth's population has been steadily decreasing, and this will probably leave about two billion people on earth. Prior to the rapture, we had seven billion.

This mission will be accomplished with an army of two hundred million spirit beings. We read that the horses had heads like lions and fire and brimstone issued out of their mouths. They kill with the smoke, fire, and brimstone.

Their tails were like serpents. These things are worse than the locust. They are horrible to look at, and they can kill you at will. I cannot imagine a man being able to fight back against these things. The men who were left did not repent of their devil worship, idol worship, murders, sorceries, fornication, and theft. Visualize the world at this point. There is no sky or stars. The seas are like blood. The surface is burned black. Billions of people have died in just a few short years, and they know that more is coming. Despite all of these things, the antichrist and his wicked followers are still obsessed with annihilating Israel. It is total madness.

The seventh trumpet proclaims that the kingdoms of the world have become the kingdoms of our Lord and his Christ. He shall reign forever and ever! God will reward his servants, the prophets, and the saints, and all those that fear his name, small and great.

There is a payday coming for all those who love the Lord. Nothing we go through in this life is comparable to the rewards laid up for us in heaven. We can get bogged down with the cares of this life and lose sight of our eternal life. Which one is most precious?

We will leave the judgments for a moment to discuss two nonrelated events in Revelation 14.

Revelation 14:14–16 says:

> And I looked and behold, a white cloud, and on the cloud sat one like the Son of Man, having on his head a golden crown, and in his hand a sharp sickle. And another angel came out of the Temple, crying with a loud voice to him who sat on the cloud, thrust in your sickle and reap, for the HARVEST of the earth is ripe. So he who sat on the cloud thrust in his sickle on the earth, and the earth was reaped.

Many preach and teach that these verses, along with verses 17–20, describe the battle of Armageddon. This is not correct. Verses 14–16 describe the "harvest" of the earth or the "wheat" as Jesus taught us in the parable of the wheat and tares. Let the wheat and tares grow together until the time of harvest. Then I will say, "Gather the wheat into my barn but gather the tares and burn them."

Jesus is waiting for the word from God to "harvest" his wheat into the barn. Then he will gather his church from among the world. Note that an angel commanded him, "Thrust in your sickle and reap, for the time has come for you to reap." Why did Jesus have to be told by God that the time had come for him to reap the harvest of the earth or "rapture the church?" Because Jesus did not know the day or hour of his return. Matthew 24:36 says, "No one knows the day nor the hour, not even the angels, but my Father only." He includes himself in Mark 13:32, "But of that day and hour no one knows, neither the angels in heaven, nor the son, but the Father only." Jesus is ready and waiting to "harvest" the earth, but God himself will have to give the order. Note that Jesus is on a cloud, and remember, we will be caught up to meet Jesus in the clouds. The harvest of the earth spoken of here is the Rapture of the church and will precede the battle of Armageddon by seven years.

Verses 17–20 do refer to the battle of Armageddon.

> Then another angel came out of the Temple which is in heaven, he also having a sharp sickle. And another angel came out from the Altar, who had power over fire, and he cried with a loud cry to him who had the sharp sickle, saying, Thrust in your sharp sickle and gather the clusters of the vine of the earth, for her grapes are fully ripe. So the angel thrust his sickle into the earth and gathered the vine of the earth, and threw it into the great winepress of the wrath of God. And the winepress was trampled outside

the city, and blood came out of the winepress, up to the horses bridles, for one thousand six hundred furlongs.

These verses refer to the battle of Armageddon and describe carnage of epic proportions. Grapes are another crop, but we see that they are thrown into the winepress of God's wrath. They are then trampled outside the city of Jerusalem. The blood comes up to the horses' bridles, about five feet deep, for 1,600 furlongs. That is about 130 miles.

These Scriptures definitely separate Jesus's coming for the church, and his second coming in power and great glory. Other Scriptures that we have already discussed prove beyond a doubt that the Rapture and the second coming are separate events. I emphasize this because there is doctrine still being taught that Jesus will not come until the end of the Tribulation. That doctrine necessitates the church to endure and survive the Tribulation. Don't believe it! Jesus can come at any time!

THE BOWL JUDGMENTS

The first bowl is poured out, and a foul and loathsome sore came upon the men who had the mark of the beast and those who worshiped the image. These foul sores affect only the followers of the antichrist.

The second bowl is poured out, and the sea became as the blood of a dead man, and every living creature in the sea died. The blood of a dead man becomes thick, black, and putrid. It is hard to visualize the seas in this condition, but there will be a solution when Jesus rules from his throne.

The third bowl is poured out on the rivers and springs of water, and all water becomes blood.

The fourth bowl is poured out on the sun, and men were scorched with fire and great heat. They blasphemed God but did not repent of their wickedness.

Men know that God is scorching them with great heat, and this, with no water to drink. These men are beyond hope of salvation, so they continue to blaspheme the God who created them. How do we reach this point? By giving into and living a life of sin.

The fifth bowl is poured out on the throne of the beast. His kingdom becomes full of darkness, and they gnaw their tongues because of the pain. They blasphemed the god of heaven because of their pains and their sores and did not repent of their deeds.

When the antichrist came to power, he implemented many laws, regulations, and decrees that were supposed to fix the world's problems. None of them worked, and now his kingdom is "full of darkness." At this point, all he can do is lick his sores and blaspheme God, and besides that, it's about to get worse.

The sixth seal is poured out on the great river Euphrates, and its water was dried up so that the way of the kings from the east might be prepared.

The great river Euphrates is dried up to prepare a way for the kings of the East. Looking east on the map, we see Iran, Afghanistan, Pakistan, and six other countries ending with "stan." We also see China to the east and Russia to the north. Evidently, if no usable roads are available, the armies of the east will simply drive down the hard, dry riverbed. I visualize it almost like a superhighway.

The Euphrates River flows by the modern, rebuilt city of Babylon in Iraq. Babylon will become a great city on the earth as it will be the headquarters for the world government. It is already substantially rebuilt, and its progress can be accessed on the Internet by simply typing in "modern Babylon". Although Babylon is a modern, new city in Iraq, it was not bothered in any way by Allied forces during the Gulf War nor during the ten-year occupation of that country by US forces. I never heard of it being fired on or bombed. In fact, I never heard of it until I researched it. Babylon is the newest city on earth that no one has ever heard about, but that will change very soon. When the sixth bowl was poured out, we also see that demon spirits went to all the kings of the earth to gather them to battle. They gathered in a place call Armageddon.

The seventh bowl is poured out into the air, and a loud voice from the throne in heaven proclaims, "It is done!" There is a great earthquake, the greatest ever, and Jerusalem is divided into three parts, and the cities of the nations fall. Every island sinks, and the mountains are not found.

A great hail from heaven fell on men. The hailstones weighed about a talent each. A talent is approximately ninety-six pounds.

Is the score beginning to even up? Lift up your heads, we are about to win! The antichrist has done all the damage that he can do, and the Lord has poured his wrath out on the earth. We are now at the end of the Tribulation and in a very narrow time slot described in Daniel 12:11–12:

> And from the time that the daily sacrifice is taken away, and the abomination of desolation is set up, there shall be one thousand two hundred and ninety days. Blessed is he who waits and comes to the one thousand three hundred and thirty five days.

One thousand two hundred ninety days, or three and a half years, from the midpoint of the Tribulation brings us to the end of the Tribulation. Again, it may not be apparent to people on earth that the Tribulation has ended. It may take a few weeks of not having plagues poured on them for it to sink in. Verse 12 then says that blessed is he who comes to the 1335th day or forty-five days after the Tribulation ends. He is blessed if he comes to that point and has maintained his testimony of Jesus Christ.

The followers of the antichrist are not blessed by coming to this point. First Thessalonians 5:3 says, "For when they say, peace and safety, then sudden destruction comes upon them, as labor pains upon a pregnant woman. And they shall *not escape*" (italics mine).

During this forty-five-day period is when the earth's inhabitants will begin to say "peace and safety," they will think their ordeal has ended. They will continue to marshal a large army against Israel and Jerusalem in order to "wipe them from the face of the earth." Then the verse tells us, "Sudden destruction comes upon them." How sudden will that destruction be? As sudden as lightning coming from the east and flashing to west. *Swoosh*, *kaboom*!

Did you hear it?

We will now follow Jesus as he flashes from the east to the west and into the battle of Armageddon. Hold on tight! You are riding a white horse, aren't you?

THE BATTLE OF ARMAGEDDON

And they gathered them together to a place called in Hebrew, Armageddon.

Revelation 16:16

The battle of Armageddon or the Apocalypse as depicted in movies and other media, as a titanic clash that destroys everything and shows enormous losses on both sides, is not correct. It is not the concept that we should have of this event. It is true that it will be the two largest armies to ever meet on earth. It is also true that the carnage wreaked on the forces of the antichrist will be unlike anything the world has ever seen. Those armies will number in the hundreds of millions and all will perish. No one will be harmed on our side. Jesus is coming with all the saints plus all the holy angels. No one following Jesus will lift a hand or be harmed. They are already in their glorified state.

It will be the most lopsided loss and win ever recorded on earth. All the armies of the antichrist will be annihilated. How huge is this army? We have already noted that spirits of demons go out to the kings of the *entire earth* and gather them to the battle of that great day. Although demon spirits do this, God is in complete control. The place is called Armageddon, and all the nations will send forces against Jerusalem and Israel on that day. Revelation 19:17–21 records the battle this way:

> Then I saw an angel standing in the Sun; and he cried with a loud voice, saying to all the birds that fly in the midst of heaven, come and gather together for the supper of the great God. That you may eat the flesh of kings, the flesh of captains, the flesh of mighty men, the flesh of horses and those who sit on them, and the flesh of all the people, free and slave, both small and great
>
> And I saw the beast, the kings of the earth, and their armies, gathered together to make war against him who sat on the horse and his army. Then the beast was captured, and with him the false prophet who worked signs in his presence, by which he deceived those who received the mark of the beast and those who worshiped his image. These two were cast alive into the lake of fire burning with brimstone.
>
> And the rest were killed with the sword which proceeded from the mouth of him who sat on the horse. And all the birds were filled with their flesh.

This enormous army is slain by the power and glory of Jesus's brilliant appearing. I visualize the destruction of the armies of the antichrist as being instantaneous.

We are told in Zechariah 14:12 exactly how they die:

> And this shall be the plague with which the Lord will strike all the people who fought against Jerusalem: Their flesh shall dissolve while they stand on their feet, their eyes shall dissolve in their sockets, and their tongues shall dissolve in their mouths.

This is not the result of an atomic bomb or nuclear weapon as many claim. It is a plague from God.

The raptured church, including all believers down through the ages who were resurrected on that day, plus those who were martyred during the Tribulation as a witness for Jesus, plus all the holy angels, will follow Jesus into the battle of Armageddon. Revelation 19:14 says, "And the armies of Heaven, clothed in fine linen, white and clean, followed him on white horses." These are fine clothes, white and clean. We will keep them that way. Our horses will also remain clean and white.

It is logical to think that the holy angels will assist Jesus at the judgment of the nations. Everyone left on earth will be judged. There will be hundreds of millions of people on both sides. These people will still be in the flesh and capable of some resistance. I will note that we are now dealing with millions of people instead of billions. The holy angels will come with Jesus, and one of their jobs may be is to ensure order on the "goat" side until they are banished to hell. Then, Jesus will say to those on his left hand, "Depart from me, you cursed, into the everlasting fire prepared for the devil and his angels."

The battle of Armageddon is over almost before it begins. Jesus is in total control. Feeble human beings attempt to fight against God and all the armies of heaven! How could they be so blinded? Jesus warned Peter that Satan wanted to "sift him like wheat." Is this what it looks like to be sifted like wheat?" James 1:14 says, "Desire gives birth to sin and when sin is full grown, it brings forth death." Sin brought forth their death. They were "sifted like wheat." During the course of the seven-year Tribulation, billions of people, blinded by Satan, will die and wind up in hell. Revelation 12:12 tells us, "Woe to the inhabitants of the earth and sea! For the Devil has come down to you, *having great wrath* (italics mine), for he knows that his time is short." We are not yet into the Tribulation, but Satan's time is already short and he is working furiously to turn people's hearts away from God. Do not get caught in his snare. Seek a deeper walk with God day by day.

Let's do a recap. The antichrist amasses his armies to fight against God. Jesus arrives with power and great glory. Every eye sees Jesus, and every tongue will confess that Jesus Christ is Lord. The beast and false prophet are cast into the lake of fire. The armies of the antichrist are annihilated. The Tribulation has ended, and the earth is in shambles. The oceans are dead with no living creatures. All rivers are blood. All green grass is burned up. The greatest earthquake ever has caused the cities of the nations to fall. Every island has sunk. The mountains have been leveled, and the sky and stars are no more. None of this deterred the antichrist from trying to "wipe Israel off the map." But now it is over, and Jesus has conducted the judgment of the nations. The wicked from those nations have been banished to hell. The righteous are the only people left. They will serve Jesus with gladness and joy.

The one thousand years of perfect rule will now begin. Can the earth go from decimated to an ideal place to live, with no war, nothing to hurt in any way, and an abundance of everything?

The answer is *yes*! In the next chapter, we will see a wonderful time on earth. It was meant to be that way from the beginning. For one thousand years, we will live the way God originally intended for us to live. It is lovely to contemplate.

1,000 YEARS OF PERFECT JUSTICE

> I will be their God and they will be my people.
>
> Jeremiah 31:33

After Jesus is seated on his throne, in the temple, in Jerusalem, there will be several priorities.

1. The earth is in total ruin and needs "healing."
2. The cities that are to be inhabited need to be rebuilt.
3. The earth needs to produce food again.
4. All of the Jewish people have to be returned to their homeland.
5. Concurrent with the above priorities will be another very urgent job that must be done—the burial of all the dead bodies from the battle of Armageddon.

Ezekiel 39:11–16 describes the burial like this:

> It will come to pass in that day that I will give Gog a burial place there in Israel, the valley of those who pass by east of the sea; and it will obstruct travelers, because they will bury Gog and all his multitude. Therefore they will call it the valley of Hamon

> Gog. For seven months the house of Israel will be burying them, in order to cleanse the land. Indeed all the people of the land will be burying them, and they will gain renown for it on the day that I am glorified, says the Lord God. They will set apart men regularly employed, with the help of a search party, to pass through the land and bury those bodies remaining on the ground, in order to cleanse it. At the end of the seven months they will make a search. The search party will pass through the land and whenever anyone sees a man's bone, he will set up a marker by it, until the buriers have buried it in the valley of Hamon Gog. The name of the city will also be Hamonah. Thus shall they cleanse the land.

It will take seven months to bury all of the dead bodies. It will be done using mass graves and modern bulldozers and earth-moving equipment. I know, I know, the word doesn't say anything about bulldozers or earthmovers. However, Israel already has the heavy equipment they need for this job. They bought most of it from America. We don't know how many died in the battle of Armageddon, but we do know that the blood was up to the horses bridles for over 130 miles. If seven hundred million died, Israel would have to average burying one hundred million per month or three to four million per day.

They cannot do it by hand. Modern equipment will be working around the clock, even on the Sabbath.

The burial job will be so immense that it will obstruct travelers on the east side of the Mediterranean Sea. Thousands of bulldozers, backhoes, and earthmovers will be used to accomplish this task. Travelers through the area will not be a priority. They will have to stay out of the way until they can be escorted safely through the work zone. After seven months, the "heavy lifting" will be over, but Israel will continue to bury bodies that are found away from the battle area.

The land is now cleansed, and the people gain renown for doing an impossible job in a very short time.

How will the ruined earth be healed? Zechariah 14:8–11 tells us of living waters that will flow from the temple in Jerusalem.

> And in that day it shall be that LIVING WATERS shall flow from Jerusalem, half of them toward the eastern sea and half of them toward the western sea;
>
> In both summer and winter it shall occur, and the Lord shall be king over all the earth. In that day it shall be, the Lord is one and his name is one. All of the land shall be turned into a plain from Geba to Rimmon south of Jerusalem. Jerusalem shall be raised up and inhabited in her place from Benjamin's gate to the place of the first gate and the corner gate, and from the tower of Hananeel to the kings wine presses. The people shall dwell in it; and no longer shall there be utter destruction. But Jerusalem shall be safely inhabited.

These waters will flow east into the Dead Sea, and west into the Mediterranean. All the seas on earth will be polluted, with nothing living in them. As these living waters flow from the temple in Jerusalem, these seas will become alive and, very soon, will teem with all sorts of fish and other sea life. All oceans and other waters, such as rivers and streams, are interconnected. It makes sense that these "living waters" will make their way all over the earth, healing everything that they touch. This is a great river that never quits flowing. Ezekiel 47:1, 5–9, 12 tells us:

> Then he brought me back to the door of the Temple; and there was water flowing from under the threshold of the Temple toward the east, for the front of the Temple faced east; the water was flowing from under the right side of the Temple, south of the altar.

Verses 2–4 discuss measuring the distance and depth of the river. We resume with verses 5–9:

> Again he measured one thousand cubits, and it was a river that I could not cross; for the water was too deep, water in which one must swim, a river that could not be crossed. He said to me, Son of Man, have you seen this? Then he brought me back and returned me to the bank of the river. When I returned, there along the bank of the river, were very many trees on one side and the other. Then he said

> to me: This water flows toward the eastern region, goes down into the valley, and enters the sea. When it reaches the sea, its waters are healed.

The waters of the Dead Sea will be healed and will sustain all kinds of edible fish. The river will continue to flow nonstop. The Dead Sea will overflow and run into the Red Sea, which runs into the Arabian Sea. The Arabian Sea joins the Indian Ocean, which joins both the Atlantic and Pacific Oceans. The Atlantic and Pacific Oceans join all other bodies of water on earth.

Verse 5 tells us, "A river in which one must swim, a river that cannot be crossed." This is a powerful river of *living water* that never stops flowing. It will eventually reach every place on earth, and verses 8 and 9 tell us that every place the waters go will be healed and live. All fish and other living things had died during the Tribulation, but now we see a "very great multitude" of fish. Verse 12 tells us that all kinds of trees used for food will grow on both sides of the river. They will bear fruit every month. Their leaves can be used as medicine. Will people need medicine during the thousand-year reign? Yes, especially in the early years as the earth recovers from the Tribulation. These leaves will heal anything that may be wrong with you.

Isaiah 35:5–7 says:

> Then the eyes of the blind shall be opened, and the ears of the deaf will be unstopped. Then the

> lame shall leap like a deer, and the tongue of the dumb sing. For waters shall BURST forth in the wilderness, and streams in the desert. The parched ground shall become a pool, and the thirsty land springs of water; In the habitation of Jackals, There will be grass with reeds and rushes.

All of this is accomplished because of the "living waters" flowing nonstop from the throne of Jesus. Everyone is healed, the land is well-watered and pleasant to live in, and there is plenty of delicious food. Note that fruit is most delicious when eaten directly from the tree. Also, it has lost none of its nutritional value. Jesus opened some of the eyes of the blind, some of the ears of the deaf, and some of the tongues of the "dumb" when he walked on earth some two thousand years ago, but in these verses, we see that everyone with an affliction will be healed. They will simply partake of the leaves in some way, perhaps, rub their eyes, ears, lips, etc., with the leaves. Healing will be available for all.

Joel 2:21–24 puts it like this:

> Fear not, O land; be glad and rejoice, for the Lord has done marvelous things! Do not be afraid, you beast of the field; For the open pastures are springing up, and the tree bears its fruit; The fig tree and the vine yield their strength. Be glad then, you children of Zion, and rejoice in the Lord your God; For he has given you the former rain faithfully, and he will cause the rain to come down for you, The

former rain, and the latter rain in the first month. The threshing floors shall be full of wheat, and the vats shall overflow with new wine and oil.

An abundance of everything when just two to three years ago, there was famine and no living thing. Again, what a difference Jesus makes! Amos 9:13–15 says it this way:

Behold, the days are coming, says the Lord, when the plowman shall overtake the reaper, and the treader of grapes, him who sows seed; The mountains shall drip with sweet wine, and all the hills shall flow with it. I will bring back the captives of my people Israel, they shall build the waste cities and inhabit them; They shall plant vineyards and drink wine from them; They shall also make gardens and eat fruit from them. I will plant them in their land, and no longer shall they be pulled up from the land I have given them, says the Lord your God.

What does it mean, the plowman shall overtake the reaper and the treader of grapes, him who sows seed? Simply put, the land will produce in abundance and continuously. Just as the fruit trees are producing every month, crops may produce in a similar manner. Example, it takes about four months for wheat to mature. People may be able to plant in any month and harvest four months later, thereby having a continual harvest. I envision us eating all of our food when it is fresh picked or newly harvested. There will be no reason to can or preserve our food as we are assured of a continuous supply. Ezekiel 36:29–31, 33–36 says:

> On the day that I cleanse you from all your iniquities, I will also enable you to dwell in the cities, and the ruins shall be rebuilt.
>
> The desolate land shall be tilled instead of lying desolate in the sight of all who pass by. So they will say, This land that was desolate has become like the garden of Eden: and the desolate, wasted, and ruined cities are now fortified and inhabited. Then the nations which are left all around you shall know that I, the Lord, have rebuilt the ruined places and planted what was desolate. I, the Lord, have spoken it, and I will do it.

They will dwell in the rebuilt cities, and the land will bring forth abundantly. The people will declare that this land has become *like the Garden of Eden*. These Scriptures are referring to Israel, but if all of Israel is becoming like the "Garden of Eden," then the rest of the earth is being blessed also, especially those nations who supported Israel during the Tribulation. The entire earth will be producing like it did prior to the curse. You remember the curse. God said to Adam, "Cursed is the ground for your sake, in toil you shall eat of it." Prior to the curse, the earth brought forth abundantly, and Adam did not have to "toil." He simply ate as he desired. Those days are coming again, and they may be here sooner than we think.

Aah! The garden of Eden! I'm ready for it! Although I will be a perfected being and not in the flesh, I will still enjoy the earth as it becomes more perfect with each passing day.

Jesus desires to bring all the dispersed families of Israel home. He will be doing all of these things concurrently. Jeremiah 31:7–14 says:

> Behold, I will bring them from the north country and gather them from the ends of the earth, among them the blind and the lame, the woman with child and the one who labors with child, together; A great throng shall return there. They shall come with weeping, and with supplications I will lead them. I will cause them to walk by the rivers of waters, (when they walk by these waters they will be healed) In a straight way in which they shall not stumble; (The highway of Holiness) Therefore they shall come and sing in the height of Zion, streaming to the goodness of the Lord, For wheat and new wine and oil, for the young of the flock and the herd; Their souls shall be like a well watered garden, and they shall sorrow no more. Then shall the virgin rejoice in the dance, and the young men and the old, together; For I will turn their mourning to joy, I will comfort them, and make them rejoice rather than sorrow.

Jesus will bring them all back to their homeland. Verses 31–34 (not printed) tells us that the Lord will make a new covenant with the house of Israel. He will put his laws in their minds and hearts. He will be their God and Israel shall be his people, and everyone will *know me* (italics mine) from the least to the greatest. I will forgive their iniquity, and I will remember their sin no more.

Ezekiel 36:24–28 is similar:

> For I will take you from among the nations, gather you out of the countries, and bring you into your own land.
>
> I will give you a new heart and put a new spirit within you. I will put my spirit within you and cause you to walk in my statutes, and you will keep my judgments and do them. Then you shall dwell in the land that I gave your fathers; You shall be my people and I will be your God.

The Lord assures Israel that he will bring them back, forgive them, put a new spirit in them, and that he will be their God. The Jewish people and everyone on earth will be Christians.

They will have believed and accepted Jesus and have the Holy Spirit poured out on them.

Ezekiel 39:28–29 says:

> Then shall they know that I am the Lord who sent them into captivity among the nations, but also brought them back to their own land, and left none of them captive any longer. And I will not hide my

face from them any more; For I shall have POURED OUT MY SPIRIT on the house of Israel, says the Lord God.

The Lord restates that he will have glory among the nations, that Israel and the gentiles shall know that *I am the Lord*, that God dispersed the Jewish people, and that he will bring them back, and then the Lord says that he will pour out his spirit on them!

What will happen when God "pours out" his spirit on them? Joel 2:28–29 says:

And it shall come to pass afterward that I will pour out my spirit on all flesh: Your sons and daughters shall prophesy, your old men shall dream dreams, your young men shall see visions; And on my menservants and on my maidservants I will pour out my spirit in those days."

This is speaking of the thousand-year reign, and we will come back here momentarily.

The church got a taste of this on the day of Pentecost when the disciples were filled with the Holy Ghost and spoke with other tongues. Peter then explained that this was what was spoken of by the prophet Joel. The infilling of the Holy Spirit, with the evidence of speaking in tongues, has been available to all believers since that day. It was the expected "norm" in the early church for the believer to be filled with the Holy Ghost. It was expected in Pentecostal churches up until about the 1990's. Few believers in today's church experience this infilling, but I will tell you, there is nothing that compares to this. The spirit of God fills every fiber of your being and takes complete control of your words and actions. It took me three days to "come down" from this spiritual high. I was eighteen years old and will never forget the experience or the day. On October 14, 1961, a rushing, mighty wind roared through me, just like in Acts 2. A few years later, I heard a fighter jet take off and realized that I heard that same roar as the Holy Spirit rushed through me. That was over fifty years ago, and I remember it like yesterday.

Jesus told the disciples to "tarry" in Jerusalem until they were endued with power from on high. I give God praise for this power that comes from on high!

Now that I've said that, let's continue with Joel's prophecy. Joel is talking about the time of the thousand-year reign. Conditions on earth during the thousand-year reign are "like the garden of Eden"—wonderful and perfect in every way. Everyone on earth is a follower of Jesus. This is the time that the Spirit can be poured out on "all flesh." All flesh can and will be filled with the Spirit during the thousand-year reign.

I realize that most church folks are of the opinion that this will happen just prior to the Rapture of the church. It is often preached that way. I believe the reason for this is that we do not consider the thousand-year reign into the mix, so the church is eagerly awaiting the Spirit to be "poured out on *all flesh.*" The truth is, in the years preceding the Rapture of the church, men will "wax worse and worse," deceiving and being deceived. A few Christians will be filled with the Holy Spirit during the pre-Rapture era, but verse 28 says, "I will pour out my spirit on *all flesh* (italics mine)." Everyone will worship and follow Jesus during the thousand-year reign; therefore, the spirit can be poured out on *all flesh.*

Let's get back to God restoring Israel to their homeland. Isaiah 43:5–7 says:

> Fear not, for I am with you; I will bring your descendants from the east, and gather you from the west; I will say to the north, give them up! And to the south, Do not keep them back! Bring my sons from afar and my daughters from the ends of the earth.

Jesus is calling the Israelites home from every "corner" of the earth.

There has been a concerted effort in Israel for several years to bring Jews back to their homeland. I support this effort financially. If you support Israel, you are promised a blessing. God told Abraham, "I will bless those who bless you, and I will curse those who curse you; and in you all families of the earth shall be blessed."

Today's effort to bring the Jewish people back to their homeland *is not* the fulfillment of Isaiah's and Ezekiel's prophecies. Israel is restoring three to five thousand people per year, and that rate of return will not get all the Jews back home. This job will be done by Jesus during the early years of the thousand-year reign. Isaiah 60:8–9 says, "Who are these who fly like a cloud, and like doves to their roost?"

Did Isaiah see airplanes bringing Israelites home to "roost?" That's the way they are coming in now, and the planes (EL AL) are gray like the clouds. Verse 14 speaks to a different issue, and we absolutely must comment on it. "The sons of those who afflicted you shall come bowing to you. Those who despised you shall fall prostrate at the soles of your feet."

The sons, or descendants, of those who afflicted the Jews. We think of Germany and the Holocaust, we think of the Arab nations who harass Israel constantly and have sworn to "wipe them off the map," and maybe, we think of ourselves, if we have ever disparaged the Jewish race. I do not remember ever persecuting anyone Jewish, but I pray to God for forgiveness anyway. David and Job both prayed for forgiveness of sins that they may have committed unknowingly.

Isaiah 11:6–9 tells us:

> The wolf also shall dwell with the lamb, the leopard shall lie down with the young goat, the calf and the young lion and the fatling together;
>
> The cow and the bear shall graze together; their young ones shall lie down together; the lion shall

> eat straw like the ox. The nursing child shall play by the cobra's hole, and the weaned child shall put his hand in the viper's den.
>
> They shall not hurt nor destroy in all my holy mountain, for the earth shall be full of the knowledge of the Lord, as the waters cover the sea.

Nothing will hurt or make us afraid during the one thousand years of peace and perfection. Incredible! Nothing will even scare us. Wow! Savage animals, lions, bears, and snakes will have a totally different nature. They will mingle with animals that they would have killed and eaten. They now eat grass and straw. They will not just be "tame." The tame lions in zoos and circuses can and will "turn on you." During the thousand-year reign, you can pet the big lions and play with the cobras. They will never hurt you, and best of all, "the earth shall be full of the knowledge of the Lord."

What will we do during the thousand-year reign? Micah 4:1–5 gives us a glimpse:,

> Now it shall come to pass in the latter days that the mountain of the Lord's house shall be established on the top of the mountains, and it shall be exalted above the hills; and peoples shall flow to it.
>
> Many nations shall come and say, come, let us go up to the mountain of the Lord.
>
> He will teach us his ways, and we shall walk in his paths, for out of Zion the law shall go forth, and the word of the Lord from Jerusalem.

> They shall beat their swords into plowshares, and their spears into pruning hooks; Nation shall not lift up sword against nation, neither shall they learn war any more. But everyone shall sit under his vine and under his fig tree, and no one shall make them afraid; for the mouth of the Lord of Hosts has spoken, and we will walk in the name of the Lord our God forever and ever.

The term "latter days" refers to the thousand-year reign. Jesus shall be exalted as he rules from Jerusalem. The peoples of all nations flow into Jerusalem to worship Jesus. I visualize this as a steady, continuous "flow" of people who are anxious and excited to worship Jesus and to learn all they can about him.

We will beat our swords into plowshares and our spears into pruning hooks. These terms were applicable in Micah's day, but we do not use swords and spears today, so how does this Scripture apply? Simply put, we will not need weapons during the thousand-year reign, but we will utilize plows and pruning hooks. The Scripture indicates that people will grow crops, gardens, and vineyards. It may only be the flesh and blood people that do this, but don't worry, if you put seed in the ground, they will produce abundantly. We will not need weapons of any type. We will use the metal in our tanks and other weapons to make farm implements.

We will learn war no more! What an incredible change! Men have always been warlike. Trust no one who looks or acts different than you. Protect your turf. Only the strongest survive. I am a retired Army veteran and I "learned war" my entire career. I fought in Vietnam in 1967–1968. What a day for humanity when no one feels a need to harm his fellow man! Wow, again! When Jesus rules on earth, the savage animals are changed and so are the savage men. No one is natured to hurt anyone or anything.

How will all these people get to Jerusalem? Isaiah 35:8–10 tells us:

> A highway shall be there, and a road, and it shall be called the Highway of Holiness.
>
> Whoever walks the road, *shall not go astray* (italics mine). No lion shall be there, nor any ravenous beast shall go upon it.
>
> But the redeemed shall walk there, and the ransomed of the Lord shall return, and come to Zion with singing, with everlasting joy on their heads. They shall obtain joy and gladness, and sorrow and sighing shall flee away.

The highway of holiness! It will lead directly to the throne in Jerusalem, and it will come in alongside the river of living waters. That also leads directly to the temple. Anyone needing any type of healing can simply partake of the leaves on their way to worship Jesus. I'm sure that everyone will also be eating the fruit. Only the redeemed of the Lord will walk on this highway. Note that everyone is redeemed at this time. Also, there is no "ravenous beast." We will come to Zion with singing, joy, and gladness.

Zechariah 14:16 tells us, "And it shall come to pass that everyone who is left of all the nations which came up against Jerusalem, shall go up from year to year, to worship the King and to keep the Feast of Tabernacles."

I must shout this from the rooftop. *There will be no other religions on earth! Everyone will be Christians and worship Jesus with enthusiasm. They will be happy and excited that Jesus is living on earth. It will be the highlight of their year, and it will not become routine, even in a thousand years!*

Everyone will go "up" to Jerusalem year by year. We often hear the expression, "go up" to Jerusalem. Jerusalem is on top of a high mountain range. The approach to Jerusalem is uphill from every direction. Therefore, we will always "go up" to Jerusalem. It makes sense to think that everyone will not go to Jerusalem at the same time, but that nations and groupings of people will go at their appointed times. This will ensure an orderly and continuous flow of people going through the temple year-round. Ezekiel 46:9 explains this flow:

> When the people of the land come before the Lord on the appointed feast days, whoever enters by way of the north gate to worship shall go out by way of the south gate; and whoever enters by way of the south gate shall go out by way of the north gate.

The flow of people will be orderly with no milling around, gawking, or idle banter. The focus will be totally on Jesus. He will enter by the eastern gateway and stand by the gatepost. As the people pass north to south or south to north, they will walk close to Jesus and worship him. If the people of the other nations only get to see Jesus once per year, I'm sure that they will greatly anticipate it from year to year.

Two more things and we will conclude our look at the thousand-year reign. They are "Beulah land" and the "Tabernacle of David." Isaiah 62:2–4 says:

> The gentiles shall see your righteousness, and all the Kings your glory, You shall be called by a new name, which the mouth of the Lord shall name. You shall be called Hephzibah, and your land Beulah; For your Lord delights in you, and your land shall be married.

During the thousand-year reign, the land of Israel will be called "Beulah land." Beulah land means married to the land. Israel and its people will be that close. I hear the old song, "Beulah land, I am longing for you." The song sings of heaven, but it is Israel that will be called Beulah land. I still like that song.

In Amos 9:11, the Lord says, "On that day I will restore the Tabernacle of David, which has fallen down." In 1 First Chronicles 16:1–6, it explains this to us:

> So they brought the ark of God, and set it in the midst of the Tabernacle that David had erected for it. And he appointed some of the levites to minister before the ark of the Lord, to commemorate, to thank, and to praise the Lord of Israel: Jeiel with stringed instruments and harps, but Asaph made music with cymbals; Benaiah and Jahaziel regularly blew the trumpets before the ark of the covenant of God.

Tabernacle means "tent," but the tabernacle of David that will be restored has to be more than a tent. It must be the form of worship that has "fallen down", or been discontinued, that will be restored during the one thousand years. Verses 4–6 tell us that King David appointed ministers to commemorate, to thank, and to praise the Lord. He appointed musicians to play with stringed instruments, harps, and cymbals. He also appointed men to "regularly" blow the trumpets. He exhorted them to raise their voice with *resounding joy*!

This type of worship was not done prior to David becoming king, and it was not continued after he died. "Normal" sacrifices were resumed after Solomon built the temple. So what is the tabernacle of David that has fallen down?

It has to be the vibrant, jubilant worship of God with musical instruments and with leaping, whirling, clapping of hands, and dancing. This is what will be restored when Jesus reigns, and we will love and delight to worship in this manner. The psalmist saw this day thousands of years ago and wrote in Psalm 47:1–9 and Psalm 48:1–2:

> Oh, clap your hands, all you peoples! Shout to God with the voice of triumph! For the Lord most high is awesome; He is a great King over all the earth.
>
> God has gone up with a shout, the Lord with the sound of a trumpet. Sing praises to God, sing praises! Sing praises to our King, sing praises! For God is the King of all the earth; Sing praises with understanding. Great is the Lord, and greatly to be praised! In the city of our God, in his Holy Mountain, beautiful in elevation, the joy of the whole earth, is mount Zion on the sides of the north, the city of the great King!

Jesus will reign from his temple in Jerusalem. There will be perfect peace on earth. We will "learn war" no more. Once savage animals will not harm us. Nothing will harm us or even make us afraid.

The river of life will flow from the temple and heal all of the earth. The fruit trees will bear monthly, and there will be an abundance of everything. God will pour out his Spirit on all flesh. We will cherish and anticipate our time to "go up" to Jerusalem, to the temple, to see and worship Jesus. We will travel the highway of holiness that leads straight to the temple.

We will worship Jesus with resounding joy. It will never get routine, not in a thousand years!

WHY? WHY?

After the one thousand years are over, Satan must be released for a little season. Revelation 20:3

Revelation 20:7–10 says:

Now when the one thousand years have expired, Satan must be released from his prison and will go out to deceive the nations that are in the four corners of the earth, Gog and Magog, to gather them together to battle, whose number is as the sand of the sea. They went up on the breadth of the earth and surrounded the camp of the saints and the beloved city. (Jerusalem) And fire came down from God out of Heaven and devoured them.

And the Devil, who deceived them, was cast into the lake of fire and brimstone where the beast and the false prophet are, and they will be tormented day and night forever and ever.

This seems incomprehensible to the human mind. We had Satan in the bottomless pit.

Everything was wonderful and going great as we saw in the previous chapter. Now, he must be loosed for a little season. Why? (This is the first why.)

Verse 8 says that he goes out and deceives the people of the nations, and here is the astounding thing, not just a few, but whose number is as the sand of the sea. We started with a few million people at the beginning of the thousand-year reign, but now, due to the "perfect" conditions for the last one thousand years, we have billions and billions.

There will probably be more people on earth at the end of the thousand-year reign than ever in history. At any rate, Satan deceives multimillions of them and gathers them against Jesus and his followers at Jerusalem. This is the last confrontation between Satan and God, and like the battle of Armageddon, it is over with before it begins.

Satan knows that he is defeated, so why go through this process? Because God is in control, and God released him for this very purpose. Gather all the people on earth that want to rebel against God and bring them to one spot.

What these people were thinking is beyond me, but someway, somehow, millions rebel. Many of the nations, especially those with Arab history, may resent Jesus ruling with an "iron hand." But it seems to be human nature to fear and rebel against God. It also seems to happen when times are "good." God warned his people in the wilderness that when they lived in houses they didn't build, eat fruit from trees they didn't plant, and drink water from wells they didn't dig, they would turn from the true God and serve other gods. This aversion of God has been in people since the original sin in the garden of Eden. Adam and Eve attempted to hide from God when, prior to the sin, he would come down and talk with them in the cool of the day. Sin separates us from God to this day. People have missed being saved because of this fear. God's spirit is calling, but we are afraid. Afraid of what? Afraid of getting close to God. We know we need to be saved. We know we don't want to go to hell.

God is calling us by his spirit, and do know this, the only time we can come to God for salvation is when he calls us. This is confirmed in John 6:44, 65, "Jesus said, no one can come to me except the Father draws him." Verse 65 says, "I say again, no one can come to me unless it has been granted to him by my Father." You must respond to the Holy Spirit when God calls you. You cannot come to God for salvation at the time you may decide. If you are a Christian, you may boldly approach the throne of grace at any time and, in fact, should "pray without ceasing."

I have strayed away from the people who rebelled at the end of the thousand-year reign, but the point is, there are some folks that want nothing to do with God. Their ending was unceremonious. The Bible tells us, "Fire came down from God out of Heaven and devoured them." Jesus did not lift a hand nor did any of the "saints." This is the end of every wicked person who ever existed. All unrighteous are now burning in hell. We will cover their final fate in the next chapter. Satan was cast directly into the lake of fire. The beast and false prophet have been waiting on him for one thousand years.

Let's recap.

Why rapture the church? To keep Christians from the "hour of trial," the Tribulation, that would test all those who dwell on earth.

Why have a Tribulation? To conclude the testing of God's people, Israel, and to rid the earth of wickedness. There is no wickedness during the thousand-year reign. Satan is loosed at the end of the one thousand years to deceive as many as he could. He deceived multimillions.

Why have a thousand-year reign of perfect peace and justice? So that mankind could live "in the flesh" as God had intended in the beginning.

Why loose Satan at the end? To round up all those who could be deceived into rebelling against Jesus. God has now subdued all enemies.

Why declare time to be no more? Why recreate this earth when it is now in "great shape?" Why judge the people in hell? Why relocate them from hell to the lake of fire? Why create a new earth and new heavens?

We are now in eternity, so I will address these whys as briefly as possible in the next chapters.

THE GREAT WHITE THRONE JUDGMENT

And anyone not found written in the book of life was cast into the lake of fire.

Revelation 20:15

Revelation 20:11–15 tells us:

Then I saw a Great White Throne and him who sat on it, from whose face the earth and the Heaven fled away. And there was no place for them. And I saw the dead, small and great, standing before God, and the books were opened. And another book was opened, which is the book of Life. And the dead were judged according to their works, by the things which were written in the books. The sea gave up the dead who were in it, and death and hell delivered up the dead who were in them. And they were judged, each one according to his works. Then death and hell were cast into the lake of fire. This is the second death. And anyone not found written in the book of life was cast into the lake of fire.

Does the judgment of all the wicked seem like a totally incredible event to you? It should. All of the unrighteous dead are in hell, and now, hell delivers them "up." Then death and hell are cast into the lake of fire. There will never be another death! The souls that hell delivered up are now judged by everything written in the books, and then verse 15 tells us, "Anyone not found written in the book of life was cast into the lake of fire."

How long will it take to judge every unrighteous person who ever existed? Actually, no time at all. Time is now nonexistent. After the earth is empty of all souls, the unrighteous are standing before God and the righteous are with Jesus, then time will end. There will be no time at the great white throne judgment. We have entered eternity.

We cannot determine the exact moment when "time is no more." Revelation 10:5–6 tells us, "An angel, standing on the sea and land, will lift up his hands and swear that time should be no longer." This Scripture may apply to the end of the Tribulation as it is included in that time frame. However, time does not end after the Tribulation. Time is kept until one thousand years are accounted for. People go to Jerusalem year by year. Fruit trees bear every month. Time does not end until after the one-thousand-year reign, and Scripture doesn't denote exactly how or when it happens. It would not be necessary, or even useful to know the exact "time" that "time" ends.

In the Scripture paraphrased above, the angel is standing with one foot on the land and one foot on the sea and declares that time is no more. This is our present earth because we read that in the new earth, "there was no more sea."

The old earth is empty of people, time is no more, and we are ready for the new earth!

I MAKE ALL THINGS NEW

> I saw a New Heaven and a new Earth, for the first Heaven and the first Earth had passed away.
>
> Revelation 21:1

Revelation 21:1–5 says:

And I saw a new heaven and a new earth, for the first heaven and the first earth had passed away. Also there was no more sea. Then I, John, saw the holy city, new Jerusalem, coming down out of heaven from God, prepared as a bride adorned for her husband.

And I heard a loud voice from Heaven saying, "Behold, the tabernacle of God is with men, and he will dwell with them, and they shall be his people, and God himself will be with them and be their God. And God will wipe away all tears from their eyes; there shall be no more death, nor sorrow, nor crying; and there shall be no more pain, for the former things have passed away. Then he who sat on the Throne said, Behold, I make all things new. And he said to me, "Write, for these words are true and faithful."

The previous earth has melted with "fervent heat" or "passed away" as verse 1 says. It is apparent that the new earth is created from the elements of the old earth, although we are not told that in the Scripture. It seems logical, and the earth we are living on now was created out of material already there.

Now we have the new heaven and the new earth, and there is no more sea. There are two possible reasons for "no more sea."

1. That would make a lot more land for people to live on. About two-thirds of this earth's surface is water.

    It is also possible that the new earth will be much larger than our present earth. We infer this because the new Jerusalem measures twelve thousand furlongs wide, long, and *high*. Twelve thousand furlongs equals about 1,400 miles, and the earth will need to be large in order to accommodate this large city, especially at 1,400 miles high. I assume that people will be living on the "top floor." I have heard a few people say that the new earth will be eighty times larger than this present earth.

    They seemed in earnest, and they may know something that I don't. Scriptures say nothing about the size of the new earth, but logic says that it may be much larger than this earth.

    There will be new heavens that comes with this new and perfect earth. This is speaking of the atmosphere, skies, and space that will surround the new earth. The new heavens are also perfect, and 1,400 miles up should be just as pleasant as surface level. Four miles high is unlivable now, but in our perfected state, on our perfect earth, with our perfect heavens, 1,400 miles up should be "just right."

2. The second reason for no more sea is that the seas will no longer be necessary to create earth's weather patterns. Likewise, there will be no more sun, "For the Lord gives them light."

The new Jerusalem descends out of heaven and is placed on the new earth. It may be the only city on earth.

Revelation 21:22–23 tells us, "There will be no Temple there, for the Lord God Almighty and the Lamb are its Temple. The city has no need of the Sun or Moon to shine in it, for the glory of God illuminates it, and the Lamb is its light." Will we miss the sun and the moon? Absolutely not! We will continually bask in the glory of our Lord, and that brightness will be far greater than the sun.

Revelation 22:1–2 tells us:

> And he showed me a pure river of water of Life, clear as crystal, proceeding from the Throne of God and of the Lamb. In the middle of the street, and on either side of the river, was the tree of Life, which bore twelve fruits, each tree yielding its fruit

every month. And the leaves of the tree were for the
healing of the nations.

This sounds somewhat similar to what we had during the thousand-year reign, but there are differences. The crystal clear river does not have to heal the land. The new earth is perfect and will stay that way. It is, however, a beautiful addition to a beautiful city. It evidently flows along side the main "street of gold," as we are told that the tree is in the middle of the street of gold and on both sides of the river.

God will dwell with us. There will be no more tears, death, sorrow, crying, or pain. *The former things have passed away*! *Behold, I make all things new*! Can we cope with all things being made new? *Yes*! We will be new also, and we will stay that way forever and ever!

God has a great plan for his people. Don't lose sight of it as you go about your workaday world. We have a great destiny, and that destiny is much closer than we may think. Christians are only "the twinkling of an eye" from being with Jesus in glory. Love his appearing, and hold fast your testimony. Jesus said that he would come back and receive us unto himself. *Receive me, Lord Jesus*!